The Life and Literary Pursuits of Allen Davenport

The Life and Literary Pursuits of Allen Davenport

With a further selection of the author's work

Compiled and Edited by
MALCOLM CHASE

Routledge
Taylor & Francis Group
LONDON AND NEW YORK

First published 1994 by Scolar Press and Ashgate Publishing

Reissued 2018 by Routledge
2 Park Square, Milton Park, Abingdon, Oxon, OX14 4RN
711 Third Avenue, New York, NY I 0017, USA

Routledge is an imprint of the Taylor & Francis Group, an informa business

A Library of Congress record exists under LC control number: 94005838

Typeset by Raven Typesetters, Ellesmere Port, S. Wirral

ISBN 13: 978-1-138-33741-1 (hbk)
ISBN 13: 978-1-138-33742-8 (pbk)
ISBN 13: 978-0-429-44238-4 (ebk)

Contents

The Nineteenth Century

General Editors' Preface

The aim of this series is to reflect, develop and extend the great burgeoning of interest in the nineteenth century that has been an inevitable feature of recent decades, as that former epoch has come more sharply into focus as a locus for our understanding, not only of the past but of the contours of our modernity. Though it is dedicated principally to the publication of original monographs and symposia in literature, history, cultural analysis, and associated fields, there will be a salient role for reprints of significant texts from, or about, the period. Our overarching policy is to address the spectrum of nineteenth-century studies without exception, achieving the widest scope in chronology, approach and range of concern. This, we believe, distinguishes our project from comparable ones, and means, for example, that in the relevant areas of scholarship we both recognize and cut innovatively across such parameters as those suggested by the designations 'Romantic' and 'Victorian'. We welcome new ideas, while valuing tradition. It is hoped that the world which predates yet so forcibly predicts and engages our own will emerge in parts, as a whole, and in the lively currents of debate and change that are so manifest an aspect of its intellectual, artistic and social landscape.

Vincent Newey
Joanne Shattock

University of Leicester

Editor's introduction

Allen Davenport (1775–1846) was a moderately important figure in British radical politics during the first half of the nineteenth century. Born in Gloucestershire, one of the ten children of an impoverished handloom weaver, he received no formal education. His political career was spent in London, but had a national dimension due to his prominence as a radical land reformer. Davenport was also among those who formed the backbone of the revolutionary underground movement in Regency London. He was an early, though critical, follower of Robert Owen; one of the first male supporters of feminist causes and of birth control; and he was an important link between the Chartist movement and the heritage of the French Revolution era. Finally he was a prolific author, political journalist and poet. Underpinning all these activities was an abiding commitment to working-class self education, but also a life-long experience of poverty.

Davenport published his autobiography in 1845, and it initially attracted much interest in Chartist circles. However, no copy appears to have survived in any British or European collection. Since it was long presumed lost, historians had to make do instead with tantalising fragments from the contemporary radical press.[1] However, in 1982–3, my friend and colleague David Goodway discovered a copy of *The Life and Literary Pursuits of Allen Davenport* in the library of Vanderbilt University, Nashville, Tennessee. The Tennessee copy was part of a large and significant (but at the time unappreciated) acquisition: the Métivier Collection. This embodied the greater part of the personal library of the influential Chartist, radical journalist and associate of Marx, George Julian Harney. It included several rarities, among them not only Davenport's *Life* but also the only surviving copy of his *The English Institutions: An Educational Poem*.[2]

This volume incorporates both works in their entirety. Some shorter works appended to the originals are also reproduced. Davenport apparently intended them to constitute definitive 'specimens of the author's style in the department of polite literature'.[3] A key problem, however, is that these specimens are exactly as he described them: *polite*. His most interesting and important work was considerably less polished than the prose and verse he chose to reprint at the end of his life. This contrast reflects the essential tension of his autobiography, and of the life of its author. Davenport was a prolific radical writer; he brought to this aspect of his work the same passion and at times revolutionary vehemence that underpinned his political activity generally. However, this was an aspect of his life that Davenport as an autobiographer was strongly inclined not to emphasise. The works he chose for republication were assessed against two criteria: his literary pretensions and the respectable radical culture of his last years. The result was far from representative of Davenport's output, and to reprint it alone would do a disservice both to the author's reputation, and to any modern reader interested in either popular politics or 'non-canonical' authors of the nineteenth century. A further and more-representative selection of Davenport's political journalism and poetry has therefore been included in this edition, containing several important but not-easily accessible items from British collections. Collectively, the works of Allen Davenport reprinted here provide a unique window on to working-class radicalism in the crowded years from Peterloo to Chartism.

Sketching Davenport's life in his own autobiography, the veteran co-operator and freethinker George Holyoake wrote:

> He will have no other biographer . . . The poet was thin, and pale, and poor. He lived about the East End, was known at every workman's political meeting, and any surplus over his personal needs arising from his daily labour, was spent in publications giving information to men of his order, whom he sought to serve.[4]

Allen Davenport has another biographer at last: my thanks are due to a number of people who have made this possible, principally David Goodway, and the Library of Vanderbilt University for providing copies of the originals of Davenport's *Life and Literary Pursuits* and *The English Institution* in its care. The high priority accorded by the Library and University to the care of the Métivier Collection has placed all historians of nineteenth-century radicalism in their debt. John Harrison first encouraged my interest in Davenport, and Joyce Bellamy and John Saville, in the course of editing my entry on him in the *Dictionary of Labour Biography*, did much to help sharpen my perception of his contribution to nineteenth-century popular politics and education. My special thanks are due, as always, to Shirley Chase.

Notes

Throughout the texts that follow, Davenport's original (and often over-lavish) punctuation has been retained. Spelling errors in the originals have likewise been left uncorrected.

1 Davenport's *Life* faded from view following the appearance of an extract in the *National Co-operative Leader* (8 and 22 March 1861). That, and a con-

temporary review in the *Northern Star*, prompted labour historians in the 1960s to search for a surviving copy: see Harrison, 1961, p. 14.

2 The background to the discovery of the collection is described in Goodway, 1984b, pp. 57–60. The collection has since been re-assembled from the Library's open shelves and catalogued: see Hambrick, 1986.

3 *Life*, p. 77 – see below p. 30.

4 G. J. Holyoake, *Sixty Years of an Agitator's Life* (3rd edition, 1893), volume 2, page 263.

THE LIFE,

AND

LITERARY PURSUITS

OF

ALLEN DAVENPORT,

AUTHOR OF THE "MUSES' WREATH," "LIFE OF SPENSE," &c.

Written by Himself.

How chequered are the paths of human life,
How small the joy, how great the care and strife!
How varied are the prospects that arise,
How many changes pass before our eyes!
And when the flow'ry landscape we pursue,
Dark clouds descend, and mock our anxious view.
Ought not these lessons of our social plan,
Teach justice and humanity to man?

LONDON:

PRINTED FOR THE AUTHOR, BY G. HANCOCK,

ALDERMANBURY.

1845.

TO

W. BAINBRIDGE, Esq.,

TOLLINGTON PARK.

THE FOLLOWING LITTLE WORK,

WITH ESTEEM AND GRATITUDE,

IS HUMBLY INSCRIBED,

BY

HIS MOST OBEDIENT SERVANT,

ALLEN DAVENPORT.

75, *Noble Street, Goswell Street,*
London.
May 1st, 1845.

The task of writing the history of one's own life is certainly a very ungracious one, but as autobiography is by no means either strange or rare, and, as I have no literary friend, that I know of, that would undertake to write the life of an individual so humble as myself; and as I have been long before the public, as a periodical writer, and the author of several literary productions of mine own; I have undertaken this little narrative to gratify the curiosity of my friends, and subscribers, and such of the public that feel an interest in "the short and simple annals of the poor."

Although I cannot astonish my reader with any very extraordinary events, or surprise him, with any wonderful adventures, I persuade myself, that the plain, simple, and authentic narrative that I am writing of the circumstances, with which I have been surrounded, and the vicissitudes which I have gone through, will not be altogether uninteresting to the public in general; and much less so to those of my own order, who will be well qualified to judge of the difficulties I must have had to encounter, and the almost impossibilities I must have had to overcome, in raising myself from such a depth of poverty and obscurity, to any thing like a literary reputation; and that too without a literary friend to encourage and instruct, or an opulent patron to sympathize with my untutored genius.

I was born May 1st, 1775, in the small and obscure village of Ewen, which is on the boundary line which separates the county of Wilts from that of Glo'ster; about three miles from Cirencester, and somewhat more than a mile from the source of the Thames, on the banks of which stream stands the cottage in which I was born. That famous river, which is only a mill stream from its source to Cricklade, in Wiltshire, is called the *Tems*, from Cricklade, to Oxford the *Isis*, and from Oxford to London the Thames, where it becomes a mighty and majestic river, bearing the wealth of all the nations of the earth, on its proud and ample bosom. Consequently I came into existence, while the revolutionary war of America was raging in all its maddening fury, and which terminated, after seven years glorious struggle, in the independence, and final separation from the mother country; and would now be, if not for that plague spot, her black slaves, the envy of Europe and the admiration of the world!

Most of the persons whom I have ever read or heard of, whose genius had raised them from obscurity to public notice, had something, more or less, of an education, and in most cases had some kind friend, or generous patron, to take them by the hand, who caused them to be introduced to that portion of society, who were well qualified to judge of their merit; and to duly appreciate their literary or mechanical productions. But in both these respects, as far as I know, I stand alone. I never was in any school, for the purpose of instruction, in all my life. I had to get the very alphabet by catching a letter at a time as I best could from other children, who had learnt them at school of some old village dame, although my father, with the exception of the parson and the squire, was allowed to be the best scholar in the village; but his whole time was occupied in one continued struggle, having had nothing but the products of his daily labour to provide for himself and his numerous family, six boys and four girls; and who instead of devoting what little time he had, after his daily labour was done, to the education of his children, was obliged to mend their shoes, or card wool for my mother to spin on the following day; for at that time the spinning jennies had made but little progress; but as they advanced every vestige of that beneficial domestic manufacture which had been a little mine of wealth to the poor cottager, was for ever annihilated; the loss of which he has never ceased to deplore. Thus has the invention of machinery sunk both the agricultural, and manufactural labourer to a state of abject slavery and hopeless misery. But let me not here be misunderstood; I do not consider machinery itself an evil, it is like water, a supreme good, if rightly directed, but in its present state it is a life destroying scourge! Whereas, were all the manufacturing machinery made public property, and made to work *for*, instead of *against* the working classes, it would be one of the greatest blessings that genius ever bestowed!

In my early childhood I took great delight in making little implements of husbandry; such as ploughs, harrows, spades, rakes, wind-mills, water-mills, &c. &c. all capable of being put into action, and performing their different operations; so much so that the wheelwright of the village stood by and saw with astonishment my little plough turn over the mould as completely as those which he himself had made.

But as I grew older, my greatest ambition was to acquire the art of reading and writing; and the method which I employed to attain that favorite object is hardly worth relating, only that it shows what ingenious devices an active mind, endowed with some sparks of nature's fire, will have recourse to, in order to facilitate its progress in the pursuit of knowledge, when instruction of every kind is so denied. The plan pursued in the first instance, was this; I learnt, as most children do, a number of songs by heart, and having acquired, as best I could, a knowledge of all the letters in the alphabet, I saved all my halfpence and bought up all the printed songs that I could sing, and began with those that appeared the most easy; my new process of education. I proceeded to match all the words in my printed songs, with those I had previously stored in my mind, and by remembering the words thus learnt, by comparing notes, I knew them again whenever they met my eye. By this method the eye became the pupil of the ear, and with both faculties combined, I made such rapid progress, that I often surprised and astonished my young companions, who could not comprehend how I obtained knowledge.

The next grand object I had in view was to acquire the art of penmanship; and by some means or other, I scarcely know how, I got hold of a written alphabet, and as the written letters were arranged in the same order as the printed ones, I was not much puzzled in making myself master of them, and my readers may be assured, that with such a thirst for knowledge, I was not long before I tried my hand at black and white. I persevered, and felt astonished at my success; and felt a strong desire to know whether it was possible, that any mortal besides myself could read and understand the productions of my aspiring pen. For that purpose I collected all my best words, arranged them in the best order I could; and after a vast deal of painful study, I produced something which I fancied resembled a letter—it was a *billet doux*. I carefully folded it up, and addressed it to *the prettiest girl in the village!* I then deposited it where I knew it would be found by a young man who had had some small degree of education, and to my inexpressible joy I soon discovered that my writing could be read and partially understood, for the young man after a world of pains read the contents of the scrawl, communicated them to his neighbours, and in a short time the poor little foundling was dragged all over the village, and was the cause of many a joke, and many a laugh among the lads, and jealousy among the lasses, on the question of, *which was the prettiest girl in the village* to whom the note was addressed.

I now considered myself almost an author; and, encouraged by the success of my first effort, I was more than ever determined to persevere in my literary pursuits. My next attempt was to write a song, for my constant reference to metrical composition, had inspired me with something like the spirit of song, and created an impression in my mind that no change of situation, or fortune in after life could obliterate. But in my attempt at poetry, I found the greatest difficulty, not having acquired a sufficient number of words for the necessary arrangement of metrical composition; but as close application, and unwearying perseverance will overcome many obstacles; I finally succeeded in my poetical undertaking, and produced my song. Having annexed to it the name of a popular tune, I stuck it up against a well known tree that stood in the middle of the village, and in a day or two I had the supreme delight to hear it sung by many a lad and lass.

Those of my young readers who have aspired to authorship, and attempted to climb Parnassus, can better imagine than I can express my joy on that occasion. The joy of Columbus when he first beheld the new world; of Archimedes when he exclaimed, Euraka, or that of Franklin when he pierced the thunder cloud, and drew down the fire of heaven! was not greater than that of the little rustic bard.

When about twelve years old, I went to live with a sort of gentleman farmer, so called from part of his land being his own, whose name was Hinton, in the character of a groom, and there I learnt in a considerable degree the art of horsemanship; I could ride my horse over the leaping bar to the height of a five barred gate with ease, and thus qualified for the chase, I sometimes rode with master tantivy after the squire's hounds.

During my stay with that gentleman, young as I was, I trained a horse to run for a saddle and bridle, and had the good fortune to win the prize. That achievement brought me somewhat into notice, and I was considered a clever little rider. At length my fame as a horseman reached the ears of a Mr. Lawrence, a veterinary surgeon of Cirencester, who got up horses into condition, as it was called, and broke in colts of all descriptions, who offered me very advantageous terms if I would come and live with him when my time was out with my old master, with which I complied. In my new situation I soon discovered that my task was not only difficult, but dangerous; for although I had become a pretty good horseman, I was not exactly prepared to mount young wild colts, that had never been backed before, which I was obliged to do at the risk of my life. By practice, however, I acquired the art of clinging to the animal in such a manner, that the most wild and restive colt could not throw me from his back without falling himself, which was once the case, and had very nearly cost me my life. The animal raised himself so high upon his hind legs, that he lost his balance, and fell completely over upon his back with part of my own body under him, which bruised my limbs and otherwise injured me so much, that I was incapable of either walking or riding for a considerable time. But nothing daunted by this accident, as soon as I could walk about, I resumed my occupation, and felt proud of my prowess in rough riding, to use a military phrase.

But about the time I am speaking of I became restless, and unhappy in my mind, I sighed for liberty, and wanted to see more of the world; and without any particular cause, came to the determination to gratify my roving propensity by leaving my situation, and trying my fortune beyond the boundaries of my native district. I prepared myself as well as I could for my romantic adventure, and appointed a certain day on which to execute my hazardous design; and about three o'clock in the morning, I got gently out of bed, leaving my bed-fellow, who was my master's apprentice, in a profound sleep; I descended the stairs, got out of the back door, the front of the house being well secured by locks and bars, clambered over the garden gate, waded through a stream of water, which separated our garden from that of another gentleman's which extended to one of the streets in the town, the walls of which, on the wings of liberty, I ascended with a palpitating heart, and launched myself into a wide world, in which I had no experience to guide, nor friendly prospect to cheer me on my way. And no sooner had I obtained the full possession of unbounded liberty, than the charms of that beautiful, and enchanting goddess, seemed to fade and wither, even in my visionary sight, and I almost wished myself back from whence I had taken so much pains to escape. Before, I wanted nothing but liberty, and now, I felt I wanted every thing but liberty!

But the Rubicon,—the garden stream was my Rubicon,—was passed, and it was folly to look back; I did not know enough of London then, even by hearsay, to attract me to the metropolis of the empire, I therefore travelled in a contrary direction, and sought the metropolis of the west, the famous city of Bristol, with some thoughts of going to sea, rather a paradoxical way of increasing my liberty! But though then very young, I was a bit of a patriot, and thought, at that time, that every thing that was undertaken by England was right, just, and proper; and that every other nation that opposed her was wrong and deserved chastisement. And that France who had just killed her king, exiled her nobles, and reviled and desecrated the Christian religion, was very wicked indeed; and I shouted "Church and King" as loud and as long as any priest or lord in the kingdom. And believed that England was not only justified, but that it was her bounden duty to put down, and if possible to exterminate such a desperate nation of levellers, blasphemers, and regicides! And that was the feeling of nine tenths of the people of England at the period of 1794.

Now, why did I not go to sea? simply because nobody asked me. If any sailor had come from any of the ships, then lying in the harbour, and invited me on board, I have no doubt I should have become a sailor myself. But though nobody asked me to be a sailor, it was not long before some body asked me to be a soldier; for a smart young corporal who commanded a recruiting party in the town, made up to me, and after describing in flourishing language the glorious cause of the war, and the delightful life of a light dragoon, proffered me the significant shilling in the name of his gracious majesty King George III. Which I, with very little hesitation, accepted, and became a soldier of a regiment of light cavalry, then being raised under the name of "Windsor Forresters." I was delighted with the name, I thought it so poetical. I had heard of Windsor forest, and that the castle was a royal residence, and became very anxious to behold the forest, the castle, and the birth place of my regiment. My desire was soon gratified, for in less than a fortnight, an order came down into the country for all the recruits to immediately join their regiment.

So after taking leave of all my friends, and addressing a little farewell poem to Anna Matilda, whom I esteemed the prettiest girl in the village, I joined my companions, and we marched from old Corinium, Cirencester, August 1794, on the very day that the right honorable Allen, Earl Bathurst, after whose name I was baptized, was borne to the tomb of his fathers, and after a pleasant march of four days, we arrived at our destination. But I did not at first find things quite so poetical as I had imagined. The temporary barracks in which the men were lodged was a miserable and filthy hole; and such a noise kept up nearly the whole of the night, that there was no getting an hour's sleep from night to morning. But I was soon relieved from that military bedlam by an order issued from the commanding officer, that all who had not had the small pox were to be innoculated; I was one who had not had that disagreeable distemper, I was therefore innoculated, with several others, and sent to Clewer green, a small village in the forest, where, having a very bad sort, I was detained many weeks, and suffered severely, being at one period of the disease quite blind; and after I had somewhat recovered, my flesh stuck to my clothes and came off by bits; so malignant was the frightful disorder with which I was afflicted. But nothing could prevent me as soon as I could walk about from taking extensive views of the beautiful forest scenes which every where met my eager eye; and which created in my youthful mind new images for poetry, and inspired a stronger passion for the muses than I had ever felt before. But before I had time to half satisfy my greedy appetite with the delights of rural scenery, the regiment received a route to march to Stamford, in Lincolnshire, where we remained a long, cold, and dreary winter. And early in the spring of 1795, we marched from Stamford to Edinburgh, and occupied new barracks, called Jock's lodge barracks. Here I found an abundance of materials for poetry. I delighted to climb up to Arthur's seat; to me it was a sort of mount Parnassus. From that elevated station, I had the most extensive views, at once beautiful and sublime; on one side were Leith harbour and the German ocean, studded with ships of all sizes, and all descriptions, going to and coming from all parts and nations of the habitable globe, gathering and distributing the merchandize of the world. From another point woods, groves, and delightful fields enchant the sight with their beautiful scenery. In another direction you have a splendid view of the rock built castle, the old, and the magnificent new town of Edinburgh. In a word, look which way you will a luxurious feast is afforded to the sight of every aspiring genius and lover of nature and art.

We remained in those barracks ten months, and the following spring, 1796, we marched from Edinburgh to the sea-shore near Dunbar, where a camp was laid out, and tents erected to receive us, and a miserable concern it turned out. Our situation in this our first encampment was wretched in the extreme; there scarcely was a dry day during the whole summer; the rain continued almost without intermission day and night; the poor horses stood shivering at the ropes, with coats all standing on end, and as rough as badgers; and the men drenched in their tents.

At that time the soldier's pay was so low, that we were literally starving. We were most of us growing youths, and had sharp appetites, and necessarily whetted by a constant exposure to the wet and the fresh air, blowing sometimes very chilly from the expansive German ocean; so that some of us, when a four pound loaf was delivered to each to serve for four days, ate more than half the first day! I and another comrade, went on a deputation to the Colonel's marquee to complain, but we could get no redress; starvation seemed to be our portion. Guess then our joy on receiving the information, that out pay was increased three pence halfpenny per day.

At the close of the summer we broke up our miserable encampment, and marched to the town of Perth, where we remained in barracks, until the following spring, 1797. There is nothing very splendid in the town of Perth, but the north and south inches, or parks, ornamented with beautiful rows of trees, and through which runs the sweet winding Tay, famous for its salmon fishery, are delightful. And in one of these inches I saw, and fell desperately in love with a young and beautiful scotch lass. It was not a "*Highland Mary*," but it was a *Highland Jane*, fair as the lily, and sweet as the opening rose. She became my inspiring Muse, the object of my adoration, and all my poetical energies, every faculty of my soul were exerted to impart immortality to, and make a goddess of my enchanting highland maid. But she was extremely bashful; and I at that time not over bold; and her parents being strongly prejudiced against the profession of arms, we had few opportunities of being together. After watching and parading round, and round the dwelling of my lovely Jane for several evenings, in order to catch a glance from her bright and sparkling eye, I was at length blessed with a momentary interview, at which we agreed to meet on the following evening in the north inch. We met, but scarcely had we seated ourselves on the green flowery bank, of sweet flowing Tay, than we heard the trumpet's angry sound echoing in every part of the town; but so attentive was I to my lady love, and so engaged by my happy feelings, that I thought the trumpeters were only practising; nor should I have attended to their call, had not two gentlemen approached us and exclaimed, "Soldier, do you not hear the trumpet sound? all your men are mounted and going to march out of town immediately." Almost frantic at this unexpected summons, I snatched a farewell kiss from the lips of my adorable Jane, and with a trembling step and a palpitating heart tore myself away from the delight of my heart and the idol of my soul! I first flew to my lodgings to collect my accoutrements, then to the stable, and in a few minutes, was in my place in the ranks. The regiment immediately filed off, and we continued to march the whole of the night; and not knowing that we should ever return, my head became bewildered, and hope, fear, doubt, love, and despair caused such a conflict in my mind, that I scarcely could have been called a rational being. Early the next morning we arrived at the ancient and castled town of Stirling, where we were stationed, we knew not for how long.

The cause of that mysterious and sudden march was the reluctance which the Scotch people evinced to being drawn for the militia, among whom many young men declared that they would rather suffer death than be made soldiers by compulsion. This little disturbance, however, was but momentary, matters were soon settled, and after a stay of three weeks we returned to our old quarters at Perth. And, oh! how different were my feelings on that happy return, than what they were on that long and dreary night, after parting with her, whose image neither time, distance, nor circumstance, could for a moment banish from my susceptible mind.

We arrived at Perth. I again saw my Jane, and was happy. But not for long, for during our stay at Perth, I and several more were seized with a dreadful fever, which carried off seven of my comrades, and left me in a most deplorable condition, so virulent was the nature of the disorder, that I became delirious, and was incapable of asking, or rationally answering a question for four weeks. And after recovery from the fever, I was subject a considerable time to fainting fits, and a frightful noise in my ears, and so reduced was I in flesh, that I never recovered it, and have been of a very spare habit ever since. During my illness, the regiment marched away from Perth, and was stationed at Montrose; where as soon as I was well enough to be removed, after taking leave of my bonny Jane, and presenting her with a farewell address, and some other little token of love, I was carried to my regiment, where the lieutenant colonel, Sir Nathaniel Duckinfield, was very kind to me; he ordered his servants to supply me with nourishing food daily, at his own house; by which kind treatment I was soon enabled to resume my military duty.

In the spring of 1798, we marched to Aberdeen, and was again encamped on the sea-shore, in the neighbourhood of that ancient city. This campaign passed away pleasant enough, having temporary stables for our horses, and the weather being favourable during the season, neither men nor horses were exposed to the hardships we had to endure in our first miserable campaign. The following spring, 1799, I was of a party appointed to escort a number of state prisoners who had been tried for high treason, having been concerned in the Irish rebellion of 1798. There were fifteen in all, and occupied five coaches. Among whom were the celebrated Arthur O'Connor, and General Ault. The former, uncle to Mr. Feargus O'Connor, the Chartist leader, and proprietor of the "Northern Star," a radical newspaper.

The destination of these prisoners was fort George, a strong fortress in the very heart of the Highlands. During our march we had an extensive view of the celebrated Culloden hills. And when we arrived at the fortress, I think we could faintly discern the city of Inverness. The fortress, as we approached it, had somewhat the appearance of a green hill, and seemed quite harmless; but when the drawbridge was drawn up, and we entered the ponderous gates, the interior presented a little town, with most formidable fortifications. Our prisoners were conducted along the ramparts, till they came opposite their place of confinement, where a temporary bridge was suspended from the rampart to the second floor of the building over which they were carried, where we lost sight of them for ever.

We remained in the fortress one night, and then returned back to Aberdeen, where we remained some time longer. During our stay at Aberdeen, I became acquainted with two young shoemakers, who worked next door to the house in which I lodged, who very pressingly invited me to come and sit by them while they were at work. I complied with their wishes, and spent what little time I had to spare in their company. They were both very ready to do me any little friendly office; and ultimately offered to teach me their trade. I was exceedingly well pleased with the kind offer of my young friends, and thankfully accepted this disinterested act of their generous friendship. I had previously learnt to make thread, and put the hairs on, and was so far master of the awl, that I could mend my own shoes, and sometimes sewed, or put patches on the shoes of my comrades.

When my young friends found that I had already been practising, they were more than ever anxious to assist me, and urged me to persevere until I had accomplished my object, which was to attempt to make a pair of shoes for myself. After a great deal of persuasion, I bought the materials, and by their direction cut them out, and commenced operations, and in the course of four or five days produced a pair of shoes, which I wore a long time, and to increase their durability, we wetted them with half a gallon of beer. I was then about twenty-two years of age, and from that moment I called myself a shoe-maker, and have followed that trade ever since.

In the year 1799, we retraced our steps, and marched back to Edinburgh, and from thence to Haddington, a few miles off this side of that metropolis, where we remained during the winter. And the following summer, 1800, we had orders to march to Warwick to be disbanded, peace having been made with the French Government.

This was a trying moment for me, and I had many severe struggles before I could decide, whether I should travel back to the north, and settle in my darling town of Perth, or march with my regiment to Warwick, and from thence return to the place of my nativity. It was entirely at my own choice, as I could have had my discharge on the spot if I had wished it. My whole heart was with my Perthian maid; with whom I had spent several happy hours on the evening of the day we stopped at Perth, during our march from Aberdeen; and whose parents after two years absence seemed quite reconciled; they not only admitted me into their house, but suffered us to be alone, and choose our own time for parting, which did not take place until a late hour; and what was further encouraging, I had received a very kind letter from her in which she apologized for the reserve, and seeming indifference, which I appeared to think she had sometimes shown; and gave me to understand that her mind was entirely made up, and hoped that mine was the same.

But I had two other powerful passions to struggle with; I had an ardent desire to see my friends and youthful companions, after six long years of absence. And although I still loved my Highland Jane, with undiminished affection, "pride, which not a world could bow," had its influence, and made me see the critical situation I was about to be placed in.

I was soon to be cast on the wide world, without being sufficiently master of any trade or calling, by which I could obtain a comfortable subsistence for myself, and much less to provide for a family. Under such circumstances what cheering prospect could I hold out to a young, beautiful, and beloved bride? Should I not have to encounter the frowns, perhaps the scorn of her parents, and friends? or what would be worse than all, I might have to sustain the loss of her affection, on whom all my peace and happiness would for ever depend. Such was the gloomy picture I drew of my prospects in the north; and I shrunk with terror from what had been depicted by a sensitive and unapprehensive mind; for though I was prepared, in some measure, to suffer hardships, and privations myself; I could not entertain for a moment the idea of causing pain to any other person; much less to her who was dear to my eyes as the light of heaven! I therefore marched with my regiment to Warwick; obtained my discharge, and pursued my course to the place of my nativity. But with a fixed determination to return to Scotland, when I had acquired a sufficient knowledge of my trade, to raise myself to the rank of an independent mechanic, and there unite my hand and fortune, with her whose image was never absent from my mind.

I shall not attempt to describe my feelings, when I came within sight of my native village. No language, no arrangement of words, can express the palpitating emotions of my heart, and the wild transports and trembling delirium that thrilled through every chord and fibre of the soul! I had no sooner entered the cottage in which I was born, than I was surrounded by scores of villagers of all ages and both sexes; nay some elderly people who had gone early to rest, actually crept from their beds, and came to congratulate me on my safe return, to "God bless me," and to express a wish for my future happiness. All this was extremely gratifying to my feelings, and if it had been possible to have had my bonny Scotch lass with me at that moment, I should have been the happiest man the world ever contained.

But the happiness I enjoyed by this revolution in my affairs, was but of a short duration; I could not get employment as a journeyman shoemaker, on account of my imperfect knowledge of the trade, and I was but ill calculated for agricultural labour; every article of consumption was excessively dear. The quartern loaf was one shilling and tenpence halfpenny, potatoes fifteen shillings a sack, and every other necessary of life in like proportion. My stock of money, which at first was only five pounds, was soon exhausted, and my prospects became more than ordinarily gloomy. And in spite of the motto which I sometimes adopted, *nil desperanda*, I was almost driven to despair. I however in the latter part of the year 1800, dropped in by accident, with a small master shoemaker, to whom I stated, in the best manner I could, the circumstances under which I was placed, and how far I had advanced in the knowledge of the trade, who after hearing my plain unvarnished tale, kindly invited me to come to his shop, which was in Cirencester, and he would see what he could do for me, in the way of putting me forward in the business. I went and he first gave me children's shoes to make, at a starvation price, but it was quite as much as he could afford, and more perhaps than my uncouth workmanship deserved. But as I worked alongside of my master, I kept my eyes wide open, and in a short time made rapid progress; so much so that within two months he gave me men's shoes to make; irons were not used then in the country; we set the stitch with the thumb nail; and in that style, I soon made a pretty good shoe, and should have got on tolerably well, had it not been for the extravagant price of provisions, which lasted nearly two years, during which time, the people in the villages of that district were literally starving.

My heart was still in Scotland; but Perth, my darling Perth! was very far distant, and I could by no means scrape up a sufficient sum to pay my carriage thither. This gave me considerable uneasiness. During my five years residence in Scotland, the land of *Burns*, I became very much attached to the Scotch people generally, who always treated me with the greatest respect. For at that time I was very religious; and often wept when I fancied I had deviated from the principles, or violated in the slightest degree the commands and injunctions of the Gospel.

During my stay in Aberdeen, I constantly attended a Methodist Chapel, where my attention was so rivetted, and my feelings so captivated by the splendid eloquence of a popular preacher, that I was almost prepared, had it been necessary, to become a candidate for the glorious and unfading crown of christian martyrdom.

In reading over the sixty-eighth psalm, I was so charmed with the splendid and poetical language in which the ideas and sentiments of the author were clothed, that I fancied I felt something like inspiration; and commenced writing a sermon; very gravely taking for my text the eighteenth verse of the said psalm; the words of which are as follows:— "Thou hast ascended on high, thou hast led captivity captive: thou hast received gifts for men; yea, for the rebellious also, that the Lord God might dwell among them." My sermon was somewhat admired by my religious friends; but the lofty, sublime, and impressive eloquence of the minister who occupied the pulpit of the chapel, so struck me with awe and admiration, that I lost all conceit of my own poor little puny production. Still I regret losing it, as it is pleasing in age to look back to youthful days, and review their early productions; especially when they are the emendations of a moral and unsophisticated mind.

I still worked on at my trade, but could make no advance, beyond a bare subsistence; and despairing of ever getting back to Scotland, I came to a resolution to take a trip to the great Metropolis, a sight of which I had had in 1794, when marching from Windsor to the North. I arrived in London in 1804, and being naturally very bashful, and also very diffident of my ability in regard to my trade, I thought it most prudent to take up my abode in some part of the suburbs; and I pitched upon the neighbourhood of Paddington. I looked about for a shop, and found one in the Edgeware Road, kept by a Mr. Harding. I walked by the shop several times, before I could muster up courage sufficient to enter it. At length however I ventured to go in and *occasion*, as we call it; and to my great joy, after being obliged to answer several necessary questions, got the grant of a seat of work, and was accommodated with a lodging in the house; I considered this a very fortunate circumstance. Still I felt great fear that my country style of work would not suit the London master, as it was not customary then to carry a shoe with you, when you applied for work. But my fears were soon dissipated, for the master saw that my work was very firm, and that was the main thing he cared about. In this situation, I soon found myself quite at home, for the master's son was an amateur in painting, chiefly in marine pieces; so that we made the two sister arts, poetry and painting assist each other, and our house became a little academy. Charles, that was the young man's name, consumed all his spare time in painting, and I mine in writing poetry, and studying music, and also giving him sketches, for I had learnt to draw a little, of harbours, piers, and rivers, for though I had never been far out at sea, I had had, while in the army, many extensive views from various parts of the shores of the great German ocean.

Charles was such an enthusiast, that I have known him to burst into tears, when he could not get on with his painting to his own satisfaction, with sheer vexation.

I was an enthusiast too, but I was more philosophical. When I could not get on in writing or in music to my wish, I imputed it to the circumstance, that perhaps I was pursuing objects that I had not sufficient genius or capacity to accomplish. I felt this so strongly with respect to music, that I never calculated on it further than for my own amusement. Poetry I could not shake off so easy; that became my ruling passion; but I felt convinced that my organ of tune was not sufficiently developed to enable me to become a professor in music.

But to return; poor Charles was soon doomed to share the fate of most aspiring geniuses, when they spring from the humbler walks of life. He fell desperately in love with, and ultimately married, a young lady of some beauty, and many accomplishments, who was governess at a school for young ladies. The prospect seemed fair; but only seemed so. He soon found that all the fine furniture, &c. that made such a grand appearance, belonged to a half crazy old aunt, who had little or nothing to subsist on, than what her pretty niece obtained from the school. His wife after marriage, grew careless, neglected her school, and lost most of her scholars; while the aunt who was cursed with an outrageous bad temper, led him a miserable life; upbraiding him with deception, she and her niece having vainly speculated upon his father being in better circumstances than he really was. He just enjoyed the common comforts of life, lived respected in his neighbourhood, and that was all. He however when the school failed set the young couple up in the green grocery and fruit line, but they spent all the money as fast as they took it, so that when the stock was all sold off, having no money to purchase more, they as a matter of course gave up shop keeping; and sunk deeper and deeper into poverty; his wife ultimately turned out to be a little vain and pert coquette, and my poor young friend, Charles Harding, became one of the most miserable of men. Doomed to incessant labour, he had no longer any time to follow the bent of his genius, in the delightful art of painting.

Misfortunes now succeeded one another rapidly in the family of that good and worthy man, my master; his only daughter was soon after married to a carpenter, who called himself a builder, who turned out to be a great profligate, and unprincipled scoundrel, who by lying tales, and false representations, induced his father in law to sign a bond for a sum of money which it was impossible that he could ever pay, should his hopeful son-in-law fail in his speculation. He did fail. And my poor old master, nearly seventy years of age, was arrested, and thrown into prison, where he caught the gaol fever and died! And Mrs. Harding, who was now left a widow, friendless and unprotected, pined and wasted away, and finally died with a broken heart! Such were the sad calamities that afflicted the first family that I knew in London.

I next worked for a chamber master, and got on pretty well by close application to business; this was in Steven's Buildings, Bell Street, Edgeware Road; where I remained a considerable time. One of this master's apprentices, a young man, on reading some of my verses, became quite enamoured with poetry, and evinced considerable genius, and tact in some of his poetical productions; and we became a sort of kindred spirits; but he died at the age of twenty four years.

This young man and myself, while we were together, took in Cooke's edition of the British Poets, then publishing in numbers at sixpence each. These standard Poets' works, especially those of Pope, were complete dampers, and went very near to extinguish every spark of my poetic genius. I felt ashamed of my own, as I now thought, wretched doggerel.

During my stay here, the man that brought our numbers, brought also a book, which he said ought to be in the hands of every Englishman in the country. The earnest and energetic manner in which the book was recommended excited my curiosity, and I purchased it; and lo! and behold! what should this wonderful book be, but the *Spencean System*? A work by the honest and indomitable Thomas Spence, containing a new administration of the landed property of the kingdom; his trial in Westminster Hall for sedition, and a great number of letters on various subjects, all calculated to improve the condition of mankind, and if reduced to practice would comparatively, make the world a paradise! I read the book, and immediately became an out and out Spencean. I preached the doctrine to my shop-mates, and to every body else, wherever, and whenever I could find an opportunity. I had been a sort of Whig Reformer before; but I now saw clearly, that all Whig, Tory, or even Radical Reformers, were as rush-lights to the meridian sun, in comparison with that proposed by the clear headed, and honest hearted Thomas Spence. And I told all the reformers that I met with, that no other reform was worth fighting for, but they generally laughed at me, and called me a visionary. This was in 1805.

The following year, 1806, I got married to a very steady and industrious woman, who was amiable in her disposition, as she was clever in her business, which was that of a dress-maker. But her business lying very wide about, and giving her great fatigue in dancing attendance on fastidious customers, she gave it up, and took to shoe binding in the women's way.

I now approached nearer the city, and got work at a shop in Red Lion Passage, kept by a Mr. Jackson, where I got two shillings and sixpence a pair at first, but I struck for wages some time afterwards, and got an additional threepence; that was considered very low wages at that time; but I had the best seat of work in the shop, in the shoe line; all my work being very light, and a great part of it pumps; and I had also the same price for boy's shoes, unless they were very small. I worked for his shop about three years; during which time, Mrs. Davenport solicited, and obtained work of Mr. Bainbridge, Southampton Court, Queen Square, and shortly after that gentleman kindly offered me a seat of work upon women's welts, or double soles, which he thought would be more profitable to me, than men's work, and we should both be at one shop. And it certainly turned out to be so, though I felt a little attachment to my friend Jackson, who appeared somewhat attached to me, for he seemed very much put out when I carried in the lasts.

I worked for Mr. Bainbridge nearly eighteen years. And it was during that time that I became a public writer, for although I had written a great number of poems of one sort or other, I had not ventured hitherto to communicate with any publication; or to print any thing myself. It was not till the 14th August, 1814, that I made my debût in the character of a poet, I then wrote a poem on the grand fetȩ in the parks, in celebration of the general peace; and sent it to the Sunday Paper, "*The News*." And on the following Sunday I had the supreme happiness to behold the poor little bantling—my first born, clad in a robe of typographical splendour, I immediately sent another poem, entitled "*The Congress*" but that was rejected. This again cooled down a little of my poetic enthusiasm; and it was not till 1818, that I made another attempt to figure in print. I had now become a desperate politician, and in the January of that year I sent a little poem, entitled "*The Topic*" to Sherwin's Register, a very fiery political publication; it was immediately inserted, and a succession of other articles followed; but it was gently hinted that pieces in prose would be preferred. I took the hint, and tried my hand in that department; and if the promptness with which all my articles were printed, be any proof of success, I was eminently successful. Sometimes I occupied half the space of the Register; and the signature of "A. D." became very popular. I attended all the great political meetings in Spa-fields, in Smithfield, and wherever and whenever any such meetings took place, whether within doors or in the open air. During the perilous years of 1818 and 1819, I strained every nerve, and called every faculty into action, to inspire the people with the spirit of Reform; and to expose the deceit, the treachery, and the base doings of the higher powers, with the Lords, and Commons, under the suspension of the *habeas corpus*. I was not content with writing to periodicals alone, I printed and published in 1819, a sort of dramatic poem, entitled "*Kings*;" or "*Legitimacy unmasked*," at my own expense. The piece was full of errors in manuscript, being written in great haste; and instead of the errors of the author being corrected, in passing through the press, they were doubled by typographical errors and blunders; but notwithstanding all its defects, the poem being written in a bold and democratic style, it became a little popular among the radicals, some of whom got it by heart, and recited, or rather acted it in small assemblies, with some applause. The booksellers thought it too strong, and refused to sell it in their shops, and whenever it was exposed, it was suppressed by the new police.

This year I became acquainted with Mr. Hunt, Dr. Watson, Thistlewood, Preston, and all the out and out radicals of that radical period. But what was most congenial to my mind, and eclipsed all other schemes of Reform, was the Spencean system, then advocated by the two Evans's, and others. They had numerous sections of disciples; but had been suppressed by a new law, and Mr. Thomas Evans and his son, were thrown into Horsemonger-lane jail; but when they were liberated from prison, the Spenceans took a place in Archer Street, Princes Street, to carry on discussions upon the same principles, but by another name. And I shall never forget the joy I felt, when going down Newcastle Street, Strand, on seeing a bill in Mr. Evans's window, directing the public to their place of meeting, and inviting people of all classes, to take part in their discussions. On receiving this information, not knowing Mr. Evans, or any other Spencean at that time, I flew away with all speed to the place named in the bill, in order to make sure of the place to which the bill directed, that I might easily find it on the next discussion night, to which I was firmly resolved to go, and to unite myself to the men, whose principles I had so long approved of, and advocated among my friends and acquaintances.

At length the evening appointed for the meeting arrived, and off I started impatient and eager, to hear what the Spenceans had to say; and no less so, to deliver my own sentiments, and express my feelings, on the subject of agrarian reform. Both the Evans's, and a great orator, whose name I learnt was a Mr. John Wright, were there. After hearing two or three clever speeches, but which I thought rather too tame, I seized the first opportunity, to deliver myself of the mass of thoughts, and Spencean ideas, that had been accumulating since 1805, in my mind. I plunged into the discussion, with all the warmth and zeal of an enthusiast; indeed I was too warm to be correct; and my maiden speech consisted of fiery and ungovernable declamations, and invectives against the present administration of landed property in England, and all other civilized nations in the world. But I was listened to with patience, and gained some applause, as the reward of my zeal; it certainly could not be for either the splendour of my eloquence, or the correctness of my logical deductions. I continued with this society, and spoke occasionally, until it broke up through a disagreement with one of the members, the much celebrated Robert Wedderburn, who took away all the forms, and got another place in the neighbourhood, which he called Hopkins Street Chapel, and in which he continued till he was arrested, tried, and convicted for blasphemy, and sentenced to two years imprisonment in Dorchester jail, where Richard Carlile was an inmate for six years.

It was in 1810, that I began to work for Mr. Bainbridge, and it was then that I first joined a shop-meeting, for all the shops that I had worked for before, were unconnected with any meetings of that kind; perhaps they were thought too insignificant to be noticed. I was kindly received by the members of the fifth division of women's men, then held at the York Arms, Holborn; and in a short time became a delegate, and represented that body for a long time. From the time that I became a member to 1813, the women's men acquired great strength as to numbers, and a considerable increase in pecuniary means. We had at one time fourteen divisions in London; besides being in union, kept up by a well regulated correspondence, with the trade in every city and town, of any importance, throughout the kingdom. But about this time the trade commenced a law suit against a master, for employing an illegal man, and refusing to discharge him. The case was conducted by two intelligent shop-mates, Messrs. Oldfield and Bent, assisted by an attorney in the court of King's Bench, Westminster. We gained the day, but the prosecution cost the trade a hundred pounds, which was money thrown away, for almost immediately afterwards the law of Elizabeth, which made it illegal for a master to employ a man in our trade, that had not served an apprenticeship, was repealed, and the trade thrown open to all.

In the spring of this year, we resolved on a general strike, for a penny on the ground work, and two-pence or three-pence on extras; which made the spring heel, with three-pence for rights and lefts, and three-pence for bespoke, two shillings, and if channells, two shillings and three-pence a pair; and every thing else in proportion. This strike was carried without a struggle. The masters made but very little objection to any of the items inserted in the statement of wages, every demand of the men was conceded, and we all returned comfortably to our work. But some of the more turbulent of the members, intoxicated with the success of our last strike, madly proposed in a few weeks after to commence another strike against Mr. Bainbridge's shop, for eight-pence extra on stitched men's double soles! which ought to have been quite out of the question, as there were not more than twenty pair of such shoes and boots made at the shop in a year. This arrogant proceedings brought on a crisis in the trade; the masters who till then had no association, and were strangers to each other, became alarmed, called themselves together, formed an association, and being completely organized, the strike was resisted, the men were defeated, and scattered to the winds; and hundreds of men, women, and children suffered the greatest privations during the following winter. From this fatal strike, I date the downfall of the power of the men, and the commencement of despotism amongst the master shoe-makers.

In 1816, I lost my wife; and in losing her I almost lost myself; she was a mild, gentle, and amiable woman, and so congenial were our spirits, and so well matched were we in disposition and habits, that we never had a serious quarrel during the ten years that we were together. And here I cannot help expressing my deep and enduring gratitude for the kindness shown, and the anxious solicitude evinced, for her recovery by Mr. Bainbridge, during the long and trying affliction, which she was made to endure. Had she been his sister, he could not have shown more tender regard, or made greater efforts to preserve her life. Many years have now rolled away, but neither time, distance, nor change, could erase from my mind, the sympathy felt, and the kindness bestowed by that gentleman, on that trying occasion; and this is all the monument I can leave, to commemorate that never-to-be-forgotten circumstance.

In 1820, when Queen Caroline, was put on her trial in the house of lords, upon the scandalous and obscene evidence collected by the infamous Milan Commission; and when the entire nation united, and rose up in her defence; having written a poem on the death of the Princess Charlotte, and the cruel treatment of her mother, by her royal husband, George IV, and his wicked and heartless tory ministry; and seven songs on the subject of her persecutions, the productions of my pen were read and sung for months, from Mile End to Brandenburgh House, the Queen's residence at Hammersmith; to where all the trades of the metropolis walked in procession to deliver their loyal addresses, in which they all fervently prayed that her Majesty, the lawful and beloved Queen of England, might triumph over all her enemies, and reign as secure on the throne, as she then lived in the heart of her people!

She did triumph over her enemies. But, alas! she perished in the arms of victory! persecution had done its work, and she died with a broken heart. But even the sacrifice of her life could not appease the malice of her persecutors, and blood was shed in her defence after death.

In 1822, Mr. Bainbridge having accumulated a considerable property, took ground in White Conduit Fields, and commenced building; building was all the rage then; and after erecting some twenty houses in that neighbourhood, he carried his speculations to Tollington Park, in the neighbourhood of Hornsey-road; where he built seven beautiful cottages, which form what is now called The Grove. At the commencement of this undertaking, I was put into the first cottage that was built, to pay the workmen, and to have an eye to the property on the premises, which was sometimes considerable; and also to manage the letting of the houses, as they were finished off; in which business I believe I was tolerably successful. I remained here about six years; during that time I worked a good portion of my time in the gardens belonging to the new cottages, and acquired a sufficient knowledge of gardening to make hot beds, to raise cucumbers, pumpkins, melons, and a variety of tender and delicate plants and flowers; by which employment my health became much improved; while the works of nature,—the rising and setting of the sun by day,—the moon,—the fixed and wandering stars that march in solemn pomp over the blue vault of heaven by night,—together with the beautiful and extensive scenery by which I was surrounded, filled my soul with raptures, and rekindled in my mind, that fond and ardent passion for the Muses, which I had so intensely felt in the days of my youth.

I now opened a correspondence with several periodicals, and dating all my articles from Tollington Park, I gave considerable publicity to that new neighbourhood, and from the idea of my living in a park I learnt that I was considered somebody of importance. And it was here, that I composed, printed and published, the romantic poem of "*Hornsey Wood*," which is now out of print; and which was favourably reviewed in some of the newspapers. At length all the cottages being let, and "Othello's occupation gone," I returned to town, and commenced working for myself, in the jobbing way, in which I have continued ever since, struggling hard for a scanty subsistence.

But I had now got into such a habit of writing both in prose and verse, that neither poverty, ill health, or any other obstacle, could check the patriotic ardour with which I burned in the cause of reform. The strong desire which I felt to see the institutions reformed, and the laws corrected, as well as to add my mite to the literature of my country, inspired me with the most exalted ideas of human policy, the most refined sentiments of the capabilities of man, and the most romantic visions of justice, liberty, and universal happiness!

In the hope of seeing these great objects accomplished, I was indefatigable in my endeavours to contribute as much as possible to facilitate the march of such principles, which were calculated to bring about the desired consummation. And in order to make my general sentiments known, I corresponded from first to last, with not less than thirty different periodical publications. But many of my literary productions were under different signatures, such as,—"*A.D.*" "*Alphus*," "*Economicus*," &c. This information I feel to be necessary, in order to qualify my critics to judge fairly of the merits, if they should discover any, and to denounce the defects, for no doubt they will find many in an author, who was too poor to employ a grammatical reader, to correct his manuscripts, and of too little importance to command the press to attend to his own corrections.

In 1826, I proposed a question, in a weekly newspaper, called the "Trades Newspaper, and Co-operative Journal," on the subject of *bread wages*; upon which a discussion was carried on for several weeks, and in which several public writers took part. I was opposed by the celebrated Mr. Francis Place, and ably supported by Mr. Hector Campbell, and others; from whose pamphlet entitled "The Impending Ruin of the British Empire," dedicated to Queen Victoria's father, the late Duke of Kent, I caught the idea of the important proposition for making *bread*, instead of *money*, the standard of wages. What is meant by making bread the standard of wages, is simply this:—mechanics and labourers would have to bargain with their employers for so many loaves per week, instead of so many shillings or sixpences; under such an arrangement, whether the price of the four pound loaf was sixpence or two and sixpence, it would make no difference in the workman's wages, as he would have the number of loaves, whatever change may take place in the meal market. If the four pound loaf was at sixpence, and his wages were twenty shillings per week, his wages would purchase forty loaves, but if the loaf was to rise to two shillings and sixpence, under the money standard, instead of forty loaves, he would be enabled to purchase only eight!! while under the bread standard, he would still have his forty loaves. This plan is still well worthy of the notice, and the consideration of the working classes of this and every other country; as it in some measure shows the mischievous working of the monetary system; and the manner in which the working man was robbed of his wages.

In the same year I declared myself in favour of what is now called the social system, in a letter published in the "Co-operative Magazine and Monthly Herald." Though I still adhered to the "*Spencean system*;" I conceived that the arrangements proposed by Robert Owen, were still more extensive and more complete, than merely causing the land to be made public property, seeing that the social system embraces all the powers of production and distribution of wealth, as well as holding the land in common, by an equitable administration of which would place all mankind *in a state of equality of condition!* And to assist in this great work of political and social regeneration, I devoted a great deal of my time in writing articles, both in prose and verse, in its defence, and in anticipation of the great happiness that would accrue to the whole human race, by the universal establishment of that paradisiacal system. And so sanguine was I, at one period, in anticipations, that I actually fancied that I should live to see it so far established, as to afford such practical lessons, that could not fail to convince both the governments of nations, and the people of the world, of the vast superiority of this system, over the old wornout institutions, corrupt and oppressive laws, and insane arrangements of present society.

In 1827, I printed and published a small volume of poems, including the one entitled "*Hornsey Wood*," under the title of the "*Muses' Wreath*," which was favourably reviewed by several of the public journals. That little work which contained only 72 pages, is now out of print, except that part which has been since reprinted in another shape, and of which I shall speak hereafter.

In 1830, being out of employ, and unsettled in my mind, owing to circumstances over which I had no control, at the wish and desire of Mr. Charles Jenneson, who had known me many years, and to whom I owe many obligations, I joined a society which was raised, and held its weekly meetings at Mr. Jenneson's, in Old-street, under the title of "The first London Co-operative Manufacturing Society." We manufactured boots, shoes, brushes, &c. and for some time, our little establishment inspired us with the most ardent hopes, that it would realize our fondest anticipations, and convince the world of the superiority of the co-operative principle over that of competition. The first superintendant of the establishment having resigned his office, I, through the interest and recommendation of my old friend Jenneson, who never lost an opportunity when it was in his power to do me a favor, was elected to succeed him. All the stores of the society were placed under my care, and a small sum of money advanced, to enable me to carry on the boot and shoe department.

At length, however, many of the members, who had been the most sanguine at the commencement, began to grow cool and flaggy, which made it necessary to propose some change in the constitution of the society. I therefore brought in a little bill of reform, which proposed that the contributions, which had been sixpence per week, should be reduced to twopence; but that every member should bind himself not to purchase any article *out*, that could be produced *in* the society. This did not appear to me, to be a very severe test. It was then discovered, however, that the customs, habits, and influences of the old society, were too much for our poor little infant community; which, after dragging on a year's existence, dissolved into its original elements, leaving nothing behind it but its name, which I have here preserved in honour of the noble philanthropists, who, with the purest of motives, and the best of intentions, founded that little society, which I have endeavoured to rescue from oblivion.

But I still remained with my friend Jenneson, and in the following year 1831; Mr. Owen having taken an extensive building in Gray's Inn Road, King's Cross, in which he established a national bazaar, in order to work out a complete reform, or rather a revolution in the commercial system of the country, and if possible of the world. We removed to that neighbourhood to be as near as possible to the grand seat of operations. The novelty of the institution excited much curiosity, and all the world seemed attracted by the rising of the new commercial star! All sorts of manufactured goods were poured into the bazaar, and which were for several weeks well supplied with bread, bacon, butter, butcher's meat, potatoes, &c. and Mr. Owen became, for a time, the golden calf of the adoring multitude. The most magnificent labour notes were issued; to which as far as taste in design, and beauty in execution were concerned, the notes of the bank of England seemed perfectly insignificant; and the business of the Exchange was carried on to a great extent.

The public mind was completely electrified by this new and extraordinary movement, and the discussions and speculations as to its success and failure were unbounded. The great assembly room, originally fitted up in the most elegant style; the walls were ornamented with flat pillars, surmounted with Ionic capitals; the ceiling was magnificently embossed, and the ornamental parts richly gilded with gold; and capacious enough to contain two thousand individuals. But all this, beautiful as that noble room then appeared, was not sufficient to satisfy Mr. Owen's ideas of taste and beauty. A splendid platform was raised, on which was placed a superb and majestic organ, at which a professional gentleman presided. Professional singers were also retained, and an excellent band of music was constantly in attendance, even on ordinary occasions. But on festival nights, no pains nor expense were spared; the whole of its avenues, were brilliantly illuminated with the most tasteful and costly Grecian lamps. Ten or a dozen musical instruments were employed; and ladies and gentlemen sung to the sweetest airs, the most celebrated and fashionable songs of the day, which excited the admiration and applause of five or six hundred supremely happy individuals, the greater part of whom, were attired in the most fashionable dresses, and bedecked with costly jewellery, which blazed in the light, and shed a glory around, which had no parallel, but in the fairy scenes of poetical romance. And many there were, whose accomplished manners, and gracefulness of deportment, would not have disgraced the drawing room of the most fastidious nobleman, in this polite kingdom.

The festivals were opened with a short lecture, on the subjects of social love, universal charity and the advantages of co-operation over the present system of individual competition. The lecture was followed by a concert, and the concert by a ball, which was generally kept up with great spirit, and the utmost good humour, till a late hour; when those happy people retired to rest, and perchance to dream of other such enchanting entertainments.

Lectures were delivered twice on Sunday's by Mr. Owen, in the great room which was always crowded to excess, and so great was the pressure for admission, that at length it became necessary to open another large room at the other end of the building, capable of containing several hundreds of people; to which a regular lecturer was appointed, and Mr. Maconnel by his eloquence and tact, never failed to draw a crowded audience. Thus were two lecturers going on at the same time and under one roof. And yet such was the attraction of that novel establishment, that hundreds of men and women, were frequently seen reluctantly retiring from the lecture rooms, being unable to obtain admission, though the price was threepence,—sixpence,—and one shilling!

Meantime every avenue to the Exchange during the whole week, was literally blocked up by the crowds of people that constantly assembled. Some attracted by the novelty of the institution, some to watch its progress, and to speculate on its success and result; some to make deposits and exchanges, and others to purchase with their labour notes, such articles that they stood in need of, or such as the stores of the bazaar could supply. But alas! it was soon discovered that the beautiful labour notes, which had been got up at a vast expense, could not by any means be forced into general circulation, on which account the supply of provisions failed, and a complete failure was the result of one of the most extraordinary movements that was ever attempted in this, or in any other country. Still the principle on which the system was founded remains unimpeachable, and ought to be cherished in the public mind.

From the breaking up of the exchange bazaar at King's Cross, my leisure time was occupied in writing the "*Life of Thomas Spence*," a play entitled the "*Social Age*," poems on various subjects, and articles in various periodicals; and in printing and publishing a little work in penny numbers, entitled the "*Patriots' Wreath.*" During which time, in 1835, I was made to endure a long and painful illness, which brought me to the very brink of the grave. And yet, after every hope had fled from my own breast, and from the breasts of my medical attendants, I recovered to the utter astonishment of every one, who had watched the progress of my disease, and the miserable condition to which I was reduced. At that time, I lodged with Mr. Newson, in Moor Lane, Cripplegate, to whose friendly offices I owe many obligations. And especially to Mrs. Newson, whose indefatigable exertions, and unwearied attention to my wants and wishes, must have contributed most materially, not only to the mitigation of my sufferings, but also to my ultimate recovery; to whom, and to Dr. Macdonnell, whose physyiological science, and medical skill in my case, proved clearly that he merited a much larger portion of encouragement and public patronage, than he at this time possessed; I owe a heavy debt of gratitude, of which this trifling acknowledgment is but a poor instalment.

After recovering from my long and severe illness, I finished my play,—the "*Social Age*," which contained all the leading principles, both physical and metaphysical, set forth in the social system; and also some opposite sentiments introduced into the dialogue, the better to illustrate and explain the views and objects of the new philosophy; in order to enable the audience, to return a fair and impartial verdict, whether for, or against the bold proposition, that, at that time, began to agitate the public mind. The play was twice represented in a theatre fitted up for the purpose, in the exchange bazaar, Charlotte Street, Fitzroy Square, before an audience of about three hundred persons, who all seemed highly delighted with the entertainment. Mr. Owen himself was present during the performance, and appeared much pleased with the piece, and the manner in which it was performed.

The following year 1836, I completed my "*Life of Thomas Spence*," which contained an outline of the Spencean system; contrasting the present system of holding and administering the landed property of England, as private property, with that which Mr. Spence proposes; which is that all the land, rivers, mines, coal-pits, &c. be made public property, and be administered on the principle of *Agrarian equality!* To abolish all sorts of taxes, whether imposed by the church or the state; to pay all church and state expenses out of the rental of the land &c., and to return the surplus, whatever it may be, in equal shares, to every man, woman, and child, in the kingdom. This plan of holding and administering the landed property of this country, is not now thought near so wild and visionary as it was forty years ago, when poor, but honest Thomas Spence, was sentenced to a year's imprisonment, and to pay a fine of twenty pounds, to the Lord, the King! A prosecution of Spence's book, which is now out of print, would be a *glorious movement*, for the working classes all over the world. I had a thousand copies of the Life of Spence, printed by Mr. R. Lee, and published by Mr. J. Cleave, of Shoe-lane, London.

This same year, I was elected president of the *Tower Street Mutual Instruction Society*, in which office I have continued ever since; and shall always feel proud of being a member of so useful and distinguished an Institution.

In 1838, I commenced printing another volume of my poems, in two-penny numbers, which were published by Mr. J. Watson, under the title of *Urania*, being an astronomical and philosophical poem, which ran through the two first numbers, and that title becoming somewhat popular, all the succeeding numbers were called *Urania*. But after getting out the first two numbers we came to a stand-still for want of means to proceed; and the work was suspended for a whole year; I being unable to meet the entire charge, as the numbers came out, and Mr. Watson appeared not inclined to risk any thing in speculating for so poor an author. As these numbers were beautifully got up, the expenses were necessarily very high. I was therefore compelled by the narrowness of my means to change my plans, and to resume my undertaking upon a more economical scale. And in 1839, being recommended by a friend, I applied to the printer of the present little work, who, although entirely differing in sentiments, kindly undertook to print my numbers at a lower price, that some greater profit might accrue to myself, and thus he assisted an humble individual, who had long been struggling with impossibilities.

In 1840, having arrived at my tenth number, I was very reluctantly obliged to rest from my labours, not for the want of matter, but through the want of means to proceed. The ten numbers, when bound up, made a neat little volume, and was favorably noticed by the public press. In 1842, however, having completed a little work, entitled "*The English Institutions*," I once more ventured to pass through the ordeal of the press; and my excellent friend Mr. H. again assisted me, and got the little work up in a most beautiful style; yet, it went off very slowly, perhaps on account of its not being properly advertised, as the booksellers consider a work cannot have a fair trial, unless some pounds are spent upon advertisements. So that literary pursuits, like lawsuits, seem to be beyond the reach of those who cannot command sufficient means to enforce their claims.

In 1844, I was elected an honorary member of the National Association, for promoting the political and social improvement of the people, held in the National Hall, Holborn. And I esteem it no small honor to be a member of such an enlightened and enlightening association, whose patriotism and literary talents are universally known and generally appreciated in England, France, America, and other nations; and the various addresses sent forth to the world on education, political and social rights, and the rights of labour, have commanded the attention, and won the respect, not only of the public in general, but the admiration of the moral, scientific, and literary world. And which, as a political body of working men, stands pre-eminent among the political bodies of the present day; being the first to take the lead in the moral movement, which is slowly, but surely and effectually, chasing away ignorance, prejudice, and political, moral, and religious error from the minds of those who do all the labour, fight all the battles, and who are the real supporters of the church, the state, the altar, and the throne!

The same year, I was elected an honorary member of the "Finsbury Mutual Instruction Society," held at 66, Bunhill Row, and which promises to become a very interesting and useful society. It is conducted by young men, with great zeal and considerable ability. The object of the members is to instruct each other, and those of their friends, who may take an interest in their proceedings, by lectures, readings, discussions, &c.

I have frequented for the last fifteen years, the Cornish Coffee House, which has made Bunhill Row so famous, and so well known, where I have been both amused and instructed. And having always found the house well conducted, and met with that kind respect and brotherly love, among the friends who are in the constant habit of meeting there to amuse themselves by public discussions, or private conversations, which is so well calculated to bind man to man, in the sacred bonds of friendship and of love, that I have always considered this house a sort of second home. And such is the force of habit, that I do not feel so happy at any other house of the same kind.

Such has been the life and literary pursuits of one, whose ruling passion has always been to acquire knowledge, and to impart it to those of his own order, who might happen to be placed at a still greater distance from the wholesome and cheering rays of that bright intellectual sun, which has now arrived at such an imposing altitude, that all the world partakes of its light, heat, and soul-stirring influence. And who, in spite of the disadvantages, under which he had to labour, and unfavourable circumstances by which he was generally surrounded, has succeeded in writing his name in the public mind, and of obtaining the approbation and respect of a considerable number of personal friends, who well deserve my most grateful acknowledgments. Among whom, Mr. William Bendall stands pre-eminent, who, under every circumstance, has stood forward as a kind patron, and generous friend. Many thanks are also due to Mr. Stephen Walker, and Mr. William Cooper, both of whom have been indefatigable in their endeavours to enforce, what they considered my claims, on the public ear, and to increase those little comforts, which are so necessary, and so soothing, in the cold and frosty winter age.

What a change has come over the spirit of this country since the days of my youth. There were no mechanics' institutes in existence then,—no mutual instruction societies,—no public libraries for the working man. But now, literary and scientific institutions, and mutual instruction societies, have sprung up, in almost every city, town, and village in the country. London alone, with its vicinity, contains nearly fifty of such very valuable and useful institutions, where persons of both sexes, and of every age, rank, and condition, have ready access to every branch of knowledge, from the first crude elements of education, to the highest branches of the most sublime sciences, at a very trifling expense! And the pleasing results are, that we see young men scarcely out of their teens, taking part in discussions and delivering lectures on subjects, where a considerable portion of learning is required, such as chemistry, geology, mathematics, and astronomy, with all the gravity, deliberation, and confidence, of old and experienced professors. And will the government and legislature of this country still look on and remain stationary, while every thing is changing around them? Will they stand still and see the intellectual struggle that is being made by the working classes, to acquire a thorough knowledge of every branch of useful science—such as the agricultural, manufacturing, and commercial systems—the principles and powers of the production and distribution of wealth—the science of government—and the best means of establishing and extending through every grade of the community, a free, and untrammelled education! Will they be the last in the race of improvement, and cling to the old worn-out laws and institutions? while inventive genius, with steam and mechanical powers, are revolutionizing every nation, and changing the political, the commercial, and manufacturing systems of the world! Are they so blind, or so infatuated, that they neither see, nor will be persuaded of the approaching storm—the moral earthquake, which will shake the world, and convulse Europe from its centre to its circumference—from the Baltic to the Mediterranean, and from the Bay of Biscay to the Bosphorus; unless an universal change in the political and social system of nations takes place, and a more equal distribution of human subsistence shall be conceded.

With the united energies of her people, and a full development of her national resources, England, under a wise, just, and paternal administration, might be raised to such a high state of physical power and moral importance, that she would be in reality, what she has hitherto been only in fiction, the envy and admiration of surrounding nations! But if the English government remains insensible to the wants of the people, and deaf to their appeals, with a legislature, too ignorant, or too corrupt, to foresee consequences, England, once the cradle of liberty,—the land of heroes,—the seat of the arts and sciences,—the grand commercial emporium of the world, and the island of enchanting beauty, will in a few years sink down into insignificance, if not into vassalage, and become an object of scorn for surrounding nations to point at in mockery, and cry,—*Behold the queen of the seas! The glory of the world!* How are the mighty fallen!

THE

FOLLOWING SPECIMENS

OF

THE AUTHOR'S STYLE

IN THE DEPARTMENT OF

POLITE LITERATURE,

ARE EXTRACTED

FROM UNPUBLISHED MANUSCRIPTS.

THE SPRING GUN

After the battle of Waterloo, in 1815, Captain B. returned to England, and lost no time in redeeming the promise which he had made, to revisit, the very first opportunity that presented itself, the fairy scenes of *Myrtle Grove*, the charming and delightful seat of his much esteemed friend, Mr. Escourt: and who thus describes the following incidental occurrences, and interesting scenes that took place during his visits, and who ultimately became a prominent actor in the sentimental and affecting little drama.

"When Mr. Escourt had recovered from his surprise, at my sudden appearance," said the captain, "he shook me affectionately by the hand, and gently reproached me for not apprising him of my arrival in the country, that he might have received me in a more suitable manner. I replied, and begged that he would waive all etiquette, as I had been too long accustomed to the plain blunt manners of the camp, to be very solicitous about the ceremonies of the drawing-room. And as I had come to see a friend, and not his side-board and equipages, I was glad that I had surprised him. Mr. Escourt smiled at my reply, and said he was happy to learn that the camp can produce philosophers, as well as heroes, for such the soldiers of Waterloo had certainly proved themselves by their cool perseverance, the patience by which they endured fatigue, and the undaunted courage and bravery which they evinced on that memorable occasion. I bowed, and was about to make some enquiry concerning Miss Stanley's bodily health, and the state of her mind, when a young lady of a most interesting appearance, stepped lightly into the parlour, made a graceful curtsey, glanced her full sparkling eyes into my face, and saluted me with a voice at once soft, sweet, and musical. I felt at the moment as if I had been under the influence of a spell; for I took the young lady who then stood before me, for Miss Stanley herself; and so confused were the powers of my mind, that I had great difficulty in stammering out a reply to the sweet young creature, who had just addressed me; and I know not how long I should have stood and looked like a fool, had not Mr. Escourt called the young lady by her name, and asked her to step into the flower-garden, and desire Miss Stanley to walk into the parlour.

"Mr. Escourt observed my confusion, and guessed at the right cause. He said that Eliza was a very good and grateful girl; for although she had never seen me before, she being at school, when the unfortunate *Theodore* was killed by the *spring gun*, she had never ceased to talk about me, and was as anxious for my return, as if I had been a fond and a beloved brother;

but while he was yet speaking, Miss Escourt returned from the garden, with disappointment painted visibly on her snowy brow, and informed her brother that Ellen was not in the garden, and at the time asked if she might step to the *bower*, and bring her home if she were there. 'No, my dear,' said Mr. Escourt, my friend and I will take a walk before tea, he will give me his opinion on the improvements we have already made in the pleasure grounds, and point out where it may be necessary to make more; we shall find Ellen at the *bower*, and we will bring her home with us.'

"I now seized the opportunity, and began to apologize to Miss Escourt, for my blundering behaviour; but the witty and fascinating girl cut me short, by exclaiming, 'Oh! Sir, it is I who ought to apologize, for having presumed to approach with so little ceremony an entire stranger, a gentleman whom I had never seen before; and the only excuse I can make is, the anxious desire I felt to see the person whom I considered the preserver of Miss Stanley's life; for whom I have always felt the tender affection of a beloved sister; and of him too, of whom my brother has so often spoken, and so highly extolled.' 'May we never again be strangers to each other,' was all the answer that I could make. She curtseyed and retired, leaving me deeper in confusion than before by this unexpected, but very gratifying compliment, which was delivered with all the magic and enchanting power of female eloquence.

"Mr. Escourt, smiling, took me by the arm, and we marched off in pursuit of the fair fugitive. We pursued a sort of zigzag rout, discussing each point of improvement, which my friend had made in his grounds, as we passed along; and so enchanted was I by the beauties of the scenery with which we were surrounded, and my mind so occupied with the young lady, from whom we had just parted, that I had almost forgotten the object of our search, till, arriving at the back of a very thick shrubbery which Mr. Escourt said was '*Ellen's bower*.' 'This,' continued he, 'is her place of retirement, whenever she can escape our vigilance, and it is here that she is to be found, when she is *non est inventus*, elsewhere.' He had scarcely finished the sentence, when our ears were saluted in the most delightful manner with the following song in a female voice, the sound of which seemed to come from the centre of the charming clump of trees, shrubs, and flowers.

SONG.

Ye Nymphs whose eyes with tears are swelling
Say, where is Theodorus* flown?
Reveal it to his faithful Ellen,
Whose bosom beats for him alone.

*Theodore was the faithful lover of Miss Stanley; and was accidently killed by a spring gun, which sad catastrophe, reduced poor Ellen, to the condition of a melancholy and moping, but harmless maniac.

By yon pale moon's cold light I'll wander,
While happier maidens sweetly sleep,
And on his absence will I ponder,
For him I'll sing, and sigh, and weep.

When with wild roses and green rushes,
My aching forehead I have crowned,
I'll seek my love among yon bushes,
Where he hides only to be found.

That he is there, I do not fear it,
Since he cannot be found at home,
I know his voice, methinks I hear it,—
Hark, hark! he calls—I come, I come.

"The air of the song was so elegiac, so sweetly plaintive, and the words so feelingly expressed, that Mr. Escourt seemed ready to die away in ecstacy, while I, though chained to the spot with undivided attention, was all impatience to behold the Nymph, Goddess, Fairy, or whoever, or whatever it was that sung so enchantingly!

"When we found that the song was either finished, or not to be resumed, Mr. Escourt flew round to the entrance of the bower, and began to caress, and compliment the fair vocalist on the beauty and skill of her performance, as he had been accustomed to do on other occasions; but instead of answering him, by throwing herself into fantastical attitudes, bursting out into a loud laugh, and joining warmly in the applause which he bestowed on her; she received him with perfect composure, and answered him in terms, at once both rational and correct.

"This unusual behaviour on the part of Miss Stanley, confounded him not a little; he drew back to a respectful distance, and stood as if doubting the evidences of his own senses, till she desired him to be seated, when he discovered that the song which she had sung so sweetly had been succeeded by tears. He made the most tender enquiries, and begged to be made acquainted with the cause of her grief. She replied that she felt herself all of a sudden very ill, but was getting better, and would soon be well. He then informed her that he had a friend waiting without, who would be most happy to see her, but as she was indisposed, he would defer the interview till a more convenient opportunity. 'Defer it not a moment,' she replied with great animation; 'pray let your friend be introduced without further ceremony; I am quite well now.'

"Mr. S. immediately stepped out, and led me to the bower, announced my name, and presented me to its fair inmate. She rose from her seat with great dignity, advanced towards me with a majestic step, and offered me her small white delicate hand. She was dressed in a loose flowing robe, encompassed round the waist with a band of green and gold; on her shoulders hung carelessly a scarf of rich Indian crape; she had on a gipsy hat, ornamented with artificial flowers, from which a black silk veil of the most exquisite workmanship, fell fantastically down the side of her snowy bosom, and gave an irresistible grace to her beautiful and elegant form; while her fine silky hair flowed down in loose light ringlets on her angelic face, and added a charm to the perfect symmetry of her delicate features.

"While Miss Stanley was pouring out her acknowledgments in the most grateful and fervent manner, for she seemed like a person just recovered from a fit of light-headedness, to recollect almost every thing that had passed, Miss Escourt, to whom the short separation from her beloved Ellen, had become painful, arrived at the bower; 'O Eliza!' exclaimed Ellen, on seeing her amiable and beloved companion, 'it is too much to behold at once, the man who saved my life, and him, (casting on Mr. Escourt a look of inexpressible tenderness,) whose whole endeavours have been employed to make that life worth preserving.' Then turning towards Miss Escourt, whose arms were already open to receive her, 'and thou, my guardian angel, who, with more than sisterly affection, hast so long and so often, watched and wept over the couch, traced the wandering steps, and pressed to thy gentle bosom thy poor bewildered Ellen! It is indeed too much:—my head swims—O my sister!'

"Overpowered by the intensity of her feelings, she sunk on the bosom of her beloved Eliza. She recovered however after some restoratives, which were very opportunely found on the spot, had been administered, and a burst of tears relieved her oppressed spirits. Mr. S. took her kindly by the hand, and gently chid her for yielding too freely to those delicate feelings, which never fail to distress both the body and the mind. But it was an effort of a grateful and affectionate heart, to relieve itself of a burden which its own sensibility had created; and he might as well have chided the waves of the ocean for dashing on the rock, against which they are sure to burst and become powerless.

"Miss Stanley, having recovered sufficient strength to walk, Mr. S. gently and tenderly led her by the shortest route, to his beautiful mansion. Leaving to me the pleasing task of attending on the lovely and fascinating Miss Escourt. I offered her my arm, which she accepted with that confiding ease, which innocence and rural simplicity, never fails to inspire.

"The chief subject of our conversation, as was natural enough, was Miss Stanley, on whose extraordinary case we expressed many hopes and many fears. And so deeply was this amiable and humane girl interested in the fate of her beloved companion, that while I expressed an opinion, that Miss Stanley, would ultimately triumph over the already abated malady, she looked into my face with such tender anxiety, while a tear of sensibility glistened in her bright expressive eyes, that she appeared to me, more like the angel of pity from heaven, than the child of humanity, and daughter of the earth. And the pleasing impression, which she at first had made, was now sunk too deep to be ever erased from the throbbing heart of her devoted conductor. And yet, although I had the most powerful desire, I could not find courage sufficient, to express a single word, which I could have wished Miss Escourt to have remembered in my absence."

THE SOCIAL AGE.

Enter Eliza. R.

John Lovewell—Oh, my sweetest girl! (flies and embraces her.) My dear Eliza! how did you learn that I was here?

Eliza.—How could I be ignorant of that of which every body else is informed? Ah! John, your popularity greatly alarms me. You have become the subject of general conversation all over this, and the surrounding villages. I fear, amidst all this tumult and turmoil of business, you will soon forget the very name of Eliza.

John. Forget Eliza! O were I to try,
T'would be in vain! for busy memory
Ne'er sleeps a moment o'er that dear name,
Or if she sleeps, repeats it in a dream.

Forget Eliza! when the gentle dove
Forgets the tender pledges of her love;
Or when the needle leaves the pole behind,
Eliza's image may escape my mind.

Eliza. (smiling,) Where did you get those pretty verses, John?

John.—Made them, love; are they not excellent?

Eliza.—If you made them, they are super-excellent. But did you really make them on me?

John.—How can you doubt it, love; do they not contain your sweet name?

Eliza.—Yes, but there are many women of that name, besides me.

John.—Oh, you little jealous thing! (caresses her.) O, Eliza, I have written a song on jealousy, should you like to hear it?

Eliza.—O, I should be delighted! Do sing it, pray?

John. From thee my heart is dead to pleasure,
My eyes are blind to others' charms,
None but thee, my bosom's treasure,
Can allure me to their arms;
And, though an hour or two I squander,
Social friendship to improve,
From thee my heart can never wander,
Jealousy's the foe of love.

Eliza—That's a sweet pretty song. How in the world have you learnt to write poetry, John?

John.—It is all owing to the ***unstamped***. If the stamp on newspapers were to be removed at once, we should all become ***gentlemen and scholars!***

Eliza.—How strange you talk to what you used to do. Pray what is it that those Londoners teach? Socialism, is it not?

John.—Yes, love.

Eliza.—Do you understand it?

John.—Not sufficiently, Eliza; but I hope we shall have it satisfactorily explained tomorrow evening, and then—

Eliza.—My master says it is a strange notion, that some of the people of London, and some other great towns, have got into their heads; and that it is calculated to overturn all the laws, institutions, and establishments in the country. And that it would ultimately destroy religion itself! Is not that sedition and blasphemy, John? Master says it is; at any rate it must be very wicked. I hope you will never think of associating with such a set of levellers, as master calls them. Master hopes that the country people will not run after men who preach such execrable doctrines! I hope you will not run after them?

John.—I shall run after nobody but you, my sweet angel, and your soul inspiring sisters Truth, Justice, Mercy, and the Muses.

Eliza.—How romantic! your head seems full of tropes, metaphors, and allegories, as my mistress, used to say sometimes to Miss Clara. Where have you been to learn all this fine talk? But I cannot stay a moment longer; I promised to return in a quarter of an hour. Now, do promise me not to join the Socialists? and then I shall be happy.

John.—Well, well, I shall see you again before the Social Missionaries arrive at Kemble, and then I will give you more information on the subject of their views and objects; and be assured that I shall advocate no system, which has not truth, justice, and humanity for its basis. Oh, Eliza! are you aware that you are fixed upon to be the *May Queen*, at the approaching festival?

Eliza.—No! What nonsense. I shall not be queen unless you are king! Will you be king?

John.—I should certainly not like any body else to be king, where you are queen, you little enchantress.

Eliza.—I must go, I must indeed.

John.—Well, love! let us walk together.

(exit both.)

END OF FIRST ACT.

NATURE AND ART.

PART I.

Almighty nature! glorious are thy works
In every part of the stupendous whole;
The earth, how beautiful! and how sublime
The fixed and wandering stars that shine above.
And the eternal sun! the sacred fire,
That through all ages unextinguished burns,
Filling Urania's temple with pure light,
And, kindling up the earth's dull atmosphere,
Gives life, and joy, and vital energy,
To sleeping dust—intelligence to man!
Who mimics nature's splendid miracles,
And calls forth new creations at his will.
The massy pyramids—the Babel towers,
And labyrinthian cities carved in rocks,
And the Colossus striding o'er the sea,
The giant wonder of the ancient world.
Palmyra—Balbeck—Babylon, and Thebes,
Were miracles of labour and of art.
The gorgeous temples of the Pagan world,
Though monuments of vanity and pride,
And dedicated to fictitious gods,
The plan and workmanship all men admire;
Stupendous magazines of sordid wealth,
Wrung from the persevering hands of industry
Which in huge heaps, like useless lumber lay,
As if to tempt some sacrilegious wretch
To plunder and destroy the noble pile.
And christian temples too of modern date,
Though dedicated to the "living God!"
And where the wretched, an asylum found,
Were not secure against a tyrant's rage,
Who trampled on divine and human laws,
To gratify his lust and savage will,
A royal brute! a murderer of Queens!
And many a ruin in this beauteous isle,
Points out the spot, and tells a mournful tale,
Where altars were profaned, and abbies fell!
Nor are the present temples so secure,
That high church priests would have the world believe.

Now free discussion dares to raise her head,
And public minds so rapidly increase,
Denouncing that which will not bear the light,
And stand the test of everlasting truth.
The arts and sciences in Egypt born,
Ere they arrived at full maturity,
Marched into Greece, a rude and barb'rous state,
Whose sons and daughters dwelt in dens and caves,
In savage life, and sought promiscuous love!
They knew not wedlock's all endearing ties,
That rivets soul to soul, in civil life,
But what cannot the sciences achieve,
When nature's inspirations warm the breast,—
Awakens slumbering thought—the latent fire,
That purges and adorns the human mind,
Which makes life worth preserving, and imparts
The means to banish ignorance and woe.
And now reclaimed by Cecrop's fostering care,
Who from their caverns called the savage tribes,
He taught them husbandry and other arts;
And instituted marriage, to improve,
Their moral, social and domestic state,
And wedded love, refined and sweetened home!
At length the sun of science rose above
The horizon of the dark mental world;
The star of Grecian genius bursted forth,
And Homer, with transcendant glory shone,
And taught the world the language of the gods!
While Phidias, with a bold unerring hand,
Carved out a god of ivory and gold;
So splendid and gigantic was its form,
It seemed beyond the reach of human skill,
And still remains a wonder of the world.
Praxeteles too, inspiration's child,
Outrivalled nature with sculptural art,
Produced a perfect beauty from a stone,
Whose face and form, and bending attitude,
Won for the sculptor everlasting fame,—
'Twas Venus, Queen of beauty and of love.
Their monuments of literature and art,
Whose grandeur tho' in ruins, strike the sight,
Like beauty sweetly smiling through her tears;
Surpassed all nations that had gone before,
And furnished models for all future time.
From Greece, the splendid arts on eagle's wings
Flew to imperial Rome! and with them bore,
Old Homer's mantle to the Mantuan swan,
Who kindled into epic fire, and sung
The second sweetest song, the world contains.

I could not refrain from inserting the following complimentary lines, which were written by an old and much esteemed friend and follower of the *Muses*; and—

Who ne'er fails to let the dull world know.
That there is *fire* as well as ice in SNOW.

"The ennobling strain—the inspiring song,
  Which are to freedom ever dear,
Were his—my friends—to him belong,
  True greatness, and a heart sincere.

" 'Twas his through many a chequered day,
  To sow the seeds of latent truth;
And *even now* its charms display,
  To approving age, and ripening youth.

"In accents mild, and manners bland—
  Yet, freedom firmly he maintains;
Hostile to fell corruption's band,
  The foe of hated slavery's chains.

"Let kindred spirits then unite
  To pour the balm; and all agree,
To do our duty, and requite,
  The bard—*the freest of the free!*"

W.S.

FINIS.

G. Hancock, Printer, Aldermanbury.

Editorial notes to *The Life and Literary Pursuits of Allen Davenport*

p. 3 *Ewen:* a hamlet within the parish of Kemble. There is no reference to Davenport's birth in the parish register. [Gloucestershire County Records Office, P186 IN 1/1.] His parents may have therefore been non-conformists, though since they apparently named him after the first Earl Bathurst (see p. 7 and note below) this would seem unlikely.

p. 7 *Windsor Forresters:* the 5th Regiment of Fencible Cavalry, formed April 1794 at Windsor, Berkshire. Fencible regiments enlisted only for home service and the duration of the war. After a brief spell in Windsor and Stamford, to which Davenport refers, the regiment was posted permanently to Scotland.

Allen, Earl Bathurst: Davenport is mistaken. The first Earl had died in the year Davenport was born.

p. 11 *peace having been made:* hostilities continued throughout this, and the following year, and the Windsor Forresters were finally disbanded after the Peace of Amiens, 1802. The date given by Davenport for his leaving the regiment is, however, corroborated by references which follow to the near famine conditions of 1800–1, 'the people in the villages of that district were literally starving').

p. 15 *Cooke's edition of the British poets:* Charles Cooke's publications were widely read and especially popular with working people because they were published in parts, 'which united a moderate price with good paper, clear printing, and tasteful embellishments,' (Thomas Carter, *Memoirs of a Working Man*, London, 1845).

p. 16 *the man that brought our numbers:* probably Spence himself (see below, p. 47). One of the earliest advocates of radical agrarian reform, Thomas Spence (1750–1814) had been born in Newcastle, the son of a poor Scottish net-maker. Most of what he learnt came from his participation in an informal group of artisans who met regularly at the workshop of a local bookbinder, among them Thomas Bewick, the wood engraver. Bewick's brother subsequently found Spence employment with Cooke in London. A prominent member of the London Corresponding Society, Spence's outspoken criticism of Thomas Paine increasingly alienated him from moderate radicals, as did his emphatic belief that force would be necessary to achieve meaningful reform. Both, however, made him the focus in the early 1800s of a small group of revolutionary radicals who later (1812) constituted themselves as the Society of Spencean Philanthropists. They refined Spence's argument in favour of public ownership to embrace 'Mines, Collieries, and many other Great Concerns'.

p. 17 *my debut in the character of a poet:* see *The News* 28 August 1814, and for the rejection of 'The Congress' ibid, 18 September 1814.

The Kings: see the further selection of the author's work, pp. 70–77

the two Evans's: Davenport is careful to make a distinction between the Spencean circle, led by Thomas Evans and his son, and the Cato Street conspirators, led by Thistlewood, whom he mentions earlier in this paragraph. However, as Davenport's own career showed (see below pp. 49–50), in practice the distinction between them was less obvious.

p. 18 *Mr John Wright:* former member of the London Corresponding Society, and a professional lecturer – a 'spouting orator', according to one Home Office spy (Public Record Office, Home Office Papers, HO 40/7). Wright was never the leader of the Spencean group, but he played a prominent part in debates.

the celebrated Robert Wedderburn: a black radical, the illegitimate child of a slave mother and a West Indian planter. Originally a Methodist preacher, he was subsequently an abolitionist, revolutionary, infidel and in his old age a brothel keeper. Davenport, a close associate at this time, shared the pulpit with him at the Hopkins Street Chapel.

p. 19 *the downfall of the power of the men:* a successful strike by the men's men in 1812 had nevertheless split their trade organisation into two districts, the City and the West End. Northampton speculators profited by this, opening warehouses in the capital and taking a large share of the export trade. The 1813 strike Davenport describes brought the masters together in a successful combination for the first time. Ten years later fewer than a fifth of shoemakers belonged to their trade society.

In 1816 I lost my wife: here, as elsewhere in the autobiography and his other writings, Davenport makes no mention of their daughter Mary Ann who had died sometime after 1816.

p. 20 *seven songs:* of these only one, a broadside ballad titled *Queen of the Isles* (see below, p. 78) appears to have been signed. It was published, as probably were the others, by John Pitts, 'the key nineteenth century printer of broadsheet ballads, chapbooks, and other ephemera . . . [and] the important link between eighteenth-century chapbook printing and the nineteenth-century revival of ballad printing', (Shepard, 1969, p. 13). Pitts operated from Great St Andrews Street in Seven Dials, the most congested and notorious slum in London. In 1820 Pitts issued Davenport's lengthy satirical poem, *Claremont; or The Sorrows of a Prince*, an elegy in memory of Princess Charlotte, daughter of Caroline and the Prince Regent.

p. 21 *bread wages:* the paper was the *Trades Newspaper and Weekly Free Press* and Davenport's proposal appeared in the 11 September 1825 issue. A further article on 4 December 1825 replied to the several critics and supporters of the idea.

p. 22 *favourably reviewed:*

> This unpretending little volume contains a collection of Poems by Allen Davenport, an humble artisan, residing at the Grove, Tollington Park . . . We do not claim immunity for every idle pretender; but we protest against that pride of learning which treats an uneducated author with intolerant insolence, and request for that author just this indulgence, – if his original merits shall exceed his literary errors, he shall be allowed to share, with his more favoured fellow-labourers, a portion of the public patronage, and not be crushed by learned criticism because fortune denied his youth the advantages of classic lore. We feel that Allen Davenport has need of the indulgence here hinted at. *Weekly Dispatch* 20 September 1829.

Charles Jenneson: Jennison, a tailor and cutter from Smithfield, and another active Spencean. In 1817 he assisted Wedderburn with the publication of a short-lived journal *The Forlorn Hope*. A co-operator and socialist, he ran the Eastern Institution in Stepney Causeway where the East London Democratic Association met in the early months of the Chartist movement. He died in 1840.

p. 24 *Mr Maconnel:* Thomas Macconnell lectured frequently to radical groups around the capital. See his *The Signs of the Times at the Present Juncture* (1835), and *The Prize Essay on 'The Present Condition of the People of this Country, and the Best Means of Improving It* (1838).

p. 25 *Mr Newson:* Charles Neesom (1785–1861), a tailor, Spencean and prominent east London Chartist. Initially Neesom was a forthright exponent of 'physical force' (he was a delegate to the Chartist Convention in 1839, and was arrested at a meeting in Bethnal Green at which arms were found in May 1840). He subsequently became a leading temperance Chartist and supporter of the 'new move'. He and his wife ran a radical newsagency and day-school in Brick Lane. In her own right, Elizabeth Neesom was a key leader of female Chartists in the capital.

p. 26 *Mr R. Lee:* Richard Egan Lee, best known as publisher (1833–4) of

The Man a lively Spencean and republican journal, and subsequently of the *English Chartist Circular*.

Mr J. Watson: James Watson (1799–1874), one of the original signatories of the People's Charter and, with John Cleave, the most important of the radical publishers of the day. Like Davenport he was active in the London co-operative movement, and in the Finsbury section of the National Union of the Working Classes.

Urania: Davenport probably took his title from the lectures of Sampson Arnold Mackey, a Norwich shoemaker, autodidact and cosmologist, who visited London regularly in the 1830s as the guest of Richard Carlile and James Watson. On these occasions he lectured at a number of radical halls and chapels. Mackay's aim (which Davenport's *Urania* reflects) was to reconcile classical, biblical, and oriental cosmology with modern physics and astronomy. The text of one of his London lectures was edited for publication by Davenport's friend William Devonshire Saull: *A Lecture on Astronomy, Adjusted to its Dependent Science Geology: in which is shewn the plain and simple cause of the vast abundance of water in the southern hemisphere* (1832). See also Mackie's *Urania's Key to the Revelation*, and *The Mythological Astronomy of the Ancients; part the second: or the key of Urania* (both published in Norwich, 1823).

English Institutions: see the further selection of the author's work below.

Mr H.: George Hancock, Printer and Stationer of 55 Aldermanbury in the City. Also the printer and publisher of Davenport's autobiography.

the National Association: founded by William Lovett to effect 'the new move' he believed necessary to Chartism. Charles Neesom was also a member and, from 1847, its secretary. Davenport greatly exaggerates its significance, both nationally and internationally.

p. 27 *William Bendall:* East End secularist and coffee-house keeper. 'Mr Davenport's constant attendant', according to the obituary in the *Utilitarian Record* January 1847 p. 1.

William Cooper: a misprint for Walter Cooper, a tailor, Chartist and freethinker, and subsequently a Christian Socialist.

Editorial Afterword

Davenport's last months

'Had he been less poor he would have been more famous', wrote the freethinker and co-operator George Jacob Holyoake in an obituary of Allen Davenport. The shoemaker had died just over a year after the publication of his *Life and Literary Pursuits*, the cause of his death, 'a tumour in the region of the stomach'.[1] There had been a flurry of interest and concern surrounding him in the final months of his life, and for this the publication of the autobiography was partly responsible. It had reminded older members of the radical movement of Davenport's contribution over thirty years, and it brought him before a new and receptive audience at a time when there was considerable interest in the land question – not least because of the launch of the Chartist Land Plan. *Life and Literary Pursuits* was treated to extended reviews in the two major labour movement weeklies, the freethinking *Reasoner* and the Chartist *Northern Star*, whilst sales of his earlier biography of Thomas Spence picked-up amidst calls for a new edition. 'It would be a concluding act every way worthy of his political life, and we are sure could be undertaken by him as "a labour of love".'[2] Davenport's health, however, was rapidly deteriorating. After presiding at a celebration in honour of Thomas Paine's birthday in January 1846, organised by Chartists in metropolitan Kent, he never again left his home. In September a public appeal was organised by Holyoake and George Julian Harney, editor of the *Northern Star*, for financial help. This 'prompt assistance and kind attention' rallied him for a while, but finally he died on 30 November at his home in Noble Street, off Goswell Road, Finsbury.[3]

A further public subscription was necessary to meet the cost of the funeral. Davenport was buried in the unconsecrated section of Kensal Green Cemetery in an unmarked common grave (plot number 6386/7). An oration was delivered by William Devonshire Saull, a City wine-merchant, freethinker and patron of radical causes. 'A greater number of friends of all shades of liberalism assembled than we have before witnessed on one occasion', ran one account, though due to earlier reports that he was to be buried in Bunhill Fields Cemetery, numbers were in fact depleted. A substantial audience, though, assembled at the Owenite Hall of Science in the City Road on the following Sunday to hear Holyoake's memorial discourse, entitled 'Why should the unbeliever fear to die?' A similar meeting was held at the Finsbury Literary and Mechanics' Institute, addressed by the Chartist tailor Walter Cooper (another freethinker, but subsequently a Christian Socialist).[4]

The purpose in reciting these details is more merely than to round off Davenport's *Life and Literary Pursuits*. Deathbed and interment were particularly important to proletarian freethinkers. On to the universal working-class concern to die and be buried with dignity was grafted a need to prove in this ultimate situation one's adherence to the cause of free thought. For infidels it was therefore a time of heightened emotional and psychological stress. In the weeks before his death Davenport had been pestered by unwelcome evangelists seeking a death bed conversion which might make useful propaganda. It was not unknown for scuffles to develop at the graveside, as Christian relations of the deceased, often abetted by a minister, sought to impose the Burial Service. Davenport had himself been involved in such an incident at the burial of the veteran infidel Richard Carlile in 1843.[5]

An atheist's burial, then, was an occasion for a show of strength and an ostentatious display of solidarity. Yet it is clear that Davenport's funeral, even by these standards, was particularly well-supported, involving a broad spectrum of radical luminaries. Those involved in the interment, collections, and subsequent memorial meetings included many prominent figures from the labour movement: Holyoake and Harney, the Chartists Thomas and Walter Cooper; the radical publisher James Watson; Isaac Ironsides, the Sheffield socialist leader; Thomas Wheeler, secretary of the Chartist Land Company; and three prominent patrons of secularism, Devonshire Saull, William Galpin and W. J. Birch.[6]

However, it is one of the several paradoxes of this autobiography that it barely hints at its author's status in the London labour movement, a status his funeral tellingly reveals. The explanation for this lies elsewhere than in Davenport having a self-effacing view of his achievements – even though he stresses in his very first sentence his consciousness that 'the task of writing the history of one's own life is certainly a very ungracious one'. Davenport's *Life*, for all its many qualities, is a problematic document: yet even its deficiencies are highly informative for the insight they can give into the mind of the author, and thus into a leading participant's assessment of early nineteenth-century radicalism and adult education.

'All working-class autobiographers', David Vincent has commented, 'by definition of their activity as autobiographers, are literate; almost all have been involved in some form of self-improvement, and thus there is a general tendency to place a high value on all forms of literature.'[7] In Davenport this tendency becomes the actual model for the work's organisation. It was written because 'I have no literary friend, that I know of, that would undertake to write the life of so humble an individual as myself; and as I have been long before the public, as a periodical writer, and the author of several literary productions.' Its continuity and coherence derive from Davenport's focusing upon his 'difficulties', and the 'almost impossibilities . . . overcome, in raising myself from such a depth of poverty and obscurity, to anything like a literary reputation.' As a result, the author's 'plain, simple, and authentic narrative', is neither simple nor wholly authentic. This becomes clearer if we reconstruct the life and literary pursuits of Allen Davenport from sources other than this autobiography.

Radicalism

According to two letters of political testimony he had contributed to the *Co-operative Magazine* twenty years before, Davenport moved in early adulthood from 'Church and King' toryism to become a supporter of the Whig Charles James Fox, leader of the parliamentary opposition to Pitt's government during the French revolutionary wars. In 1806, disgusted by Fox's behaviour once in office, he transferred his loyalties to Francis Burdett.[8] Davenport might well have persisted, as did many artisan radicals, in an uncritical attachment to the MP for Westminster had it not been for the effect – remarkably akin to religious conversion – of reading a pamphlet by the agrarian reformer Thomas Spence. Among the puzzling features of the *Life and Literary Pursuits* is the vivid, even moving, description of this experience in 1805, followed only four paragraphs later by an explicit statement that Davenport only 'became acquainted' with other Spenceans in 1819. Yet the printer's number carrier (deliveryman) who sold him that pamphlet was almost certainly none other than Spence himself. The latter had worked intermittently for the publisher Charles Cooke since 1788. Could Davenport have been unaware of his identity? Though possible, it is most unlikely: Spence was one of the great characters of metropolitan radicalism. Little more than four feet tall, a broad Geordie with a speech impediment, Spence was a pivotal figure in ultra-radical politics and Davenport was to become his most influential biographer. Indeed, Davenport's political and journalistic reputation would be founded on his bringing Spence before a new audience. Even had he been unaware of Spence's identity at the time, it seems inconceivable that he would not subsequently have realised it. At several points in his autobiography one senses that Davenport wished to distance himself, if not from Spenceanism, then from the Spenceans. The circumstances of his introduction to Spence are the first point at which he does so.

This sensation is reinforced by Davenport's handling of the years 1814–20. It is worth noting that his 'first born poem', *A Last Thought on the Fete* (p. 17) was itself a satirical attack on the Peace Celebrations of 1814; and that his second, *The Congress*, which he mentions as having been rejected, was actually refused because of the undisguised 'libelous nature' of its remarks on the Prince Regent. Yet in the autobiography Davenport is studiously non-commital about the political nature of them both, also ignoring a further early poem printed in the spirited radical weekly *Diligent Observer* in August 1817.[9] This is not to deny the subsequent influence of William Sherwin on his development as a writer, which Davenport stresses, but simply to point out that he commenced political writing rather earlier than the autobiography implies.

It is possible that his disenchantment with trades unionism after 1813 was partly responsible for his heightened interest in political radicalism. It may likewise have encouraged him to join the Spencean Philanthropists, assuming he had not already done so, for it was this group which organised two significant reform gatherings which Davenport admits attending: the first and second Spa Fields meetings of December 1816. By 1818 Davenport was a regular attender at their Soho meeting room in Archer Street. Furthermore he had rapidly established himself as a political journalist, as the first two items in the further selection of his work printed below reveal.

In 1819, far from accidentally stumbling upon the Society of Spencean Philanthropists, as he would have the reader believe, Davenport was already a well-established member of the group. In fact he had assumed a prominent role, and as a public speaker was sufficiently outspoken to have found it expedient to use the name Ferguson as an alias in case he fell foul of authority. In the spring of that year, following a split in the Spencean leadership, Davenport followed the black tailor Robert Wedderburn to form another infidel chapel in Hopkins Street, Soho. The autobiography's treatment of the events which followed is, to say the least, oblique, with no indication that the writer was a close associate of Wedderburn.[10]

As the events of 1819 unfolded, Davenport completed what might be termed his political apprenticeship. Incensed by 'Peterloo', the infamous incident at Manchester on 16 August, he immediately cast off his alias to castigate not just the authorities' handling of the situation, but the political system itself. Though almost bereft of punctuation, this Home Office spy's account vividly conveys the dramatic force of Davenport's oratory. Monarchy and aristocracy

> buy and sell you as they did living stock; this it was well known they were in the habit of doing for years they took pains when they had you in their hands to dispose of you to advantage let us then as they are within our grasp dispose of them, war as I observed on a former evening has already been declared why then should we hesitate, for

> my own part I am ready now, but let us wait 'till parliament meets is the cry of some few but what will they meet for? Why to pass a Bill of Indemnity for those Murderers the Magistrates and Yeomanry of Manchester, the adjourning of the Coroners Inquest at Oldham was sufficient to tell them that; it was evident that they dreaded a verdict of Wilful Murder; [then] where would be the Regent's Vote of thanks. The Yeomanry had murdered our fellow Countrymen but had we even in our own Defence shot one or two of them it would have been called Murder and Rebellion, but [we] will put up with it no longer. I compare the present time to the crisis of the French Revolution, we must arm ourselves as they did and in open Day too and though we may loose a few lives in the onset yet what is the army compared to the Mass of the Country who are labouring under the yoke of Despotism.
>
> ... what have we to fear from these Yeomanry they are but few compared with us and it only wants the People to make up their minds as one Man for it is better to Die fighting in the cause of Liberty and freedom than be starved by our Oppressors.[11]

This robustness of language and sentiment, so starkly contrasting with the style and content of his autobiography, is typical of Davenport at this time. A police informer observed of him and Wedderburn: 'Both orators and Audience were (with few exceptions) persons of the very lowest description. Wedderburn spoke very violently but the other person I think went even a greater length – Indeed some of their expressions appeared to have shocked even the worst of their hearers.'[12] Posterity has the police to thank for the survival of Davenport's 1819 mock epic *The Kings; Or Legitimacy Unmasked*, reproduced below from a copy in Home Office files.

Wedderburn and Davenport backed their outspokenness with a readiness for direct action. Hopkins Street became the head-quarters, with Wedderburn as its 'captain', of the sixth section of Dr James Watson's General Union of the Non-Represented People. In the closing months of 1819 the 'Chapel' also became a significant centre of armed drilling. Having infiltrated the preparations that would culminate in January 1820 in the exposure of the Cato Street Conspiracy to assassinate the Cabinet, a spy reported that, 'Thislewood [sic] says he depends more on Wedderburn's division for being armed than all the rest.' Intelligence such as this suggests that Davenport was implicated in the events surrounding Cato Street. From its inception it had been a scheme inspired by the Spenceans. Furthermore, shoemakers' trade societies throughout the capital had been poised to lend their support to the group led by Thistlewood: many years later several members of the trade surfaced, independently of each other, admitting complicity in the conspiracy.[13] Yet none were as centrally placed in the affairs of the Spenceans as Davenport, nor as closely acquainted with the main protagonists of Cato Street. However, they were no longer active radicals. It is hardly surprising that *The Life and Literary Pursuits* maintains a studied silence about the extent of its author's association with Wedderburn and Thistlewood; nor that Davenport chose to minimise his connections with Spenceanism in general during these years.

Less-readily explained, however, is the unemphatic treatment of other aspects of his political activities – his support of Henry Hunt, of militant atheism, and particularly of Chartism. These issues take us closer to the heart of Davenport's assessment of his life and times. His attitude to Hunt is relatively a minor issue, for the extent to which the memory and influence of the 'Orator' remained relevant to London politics in the 1840s can be exaggerated. Davenport's view of Hunt hardened after 1819, following the latter's contemptuous treatment of the Spenceans at the metropolitan reception they organised in his honour after Peterloo. Davenport said as much in 1831: however his admiration had once been unfettered for Hunt, the one politician 'who steers no shuffling course.'[14]

In the early 1820s, with organised Spenceanism in disarray, in the wake of internal disputes no less than Cato Street, Allen Davenport concentrated his political and journalistic energies elsewhere. As he relates in the autobiography he contributed broadside ballads to the Queen Caroline affair. *Queen of the Isles*, the only one of these he signed, is reproduced in this volume. Much of his time was devoted to Richard Carlile's *Republican*, thus confirming a commitment to freethought first evident in his speeches at Hopkins Street. As a political journalist he wrote more for this weekly journal than for any other publication, contributing during the period 1822–6 substantial articles on agrarianism, theology, women's rights, and that 'old harlot' monarchy. He was among the earliest *male* supporters of feminist causes; and it was Davenport rather than Carlile who first advocated birth control, significantly doing so in appreciation of women's desire to control their own fertility. Later he argued for female suffrage and, in line with Robert Owen's views on marriage, advocated the removal of 'family restraint . . . which has for so long held the softer sex in subjugation and slavery!' He frequently spoke at meetings of women's organisations in the capital during his career as a lecturer which took him all over London. His status in the secularist movement is apparent in his election as auditor to the Anti-Persecution Union, formed in 1843 to assist freethinkers facing trial or imprisonment, and their families.[15]

In secularism as elsewhere, however, Davenport's most significant contribution was made as a popular lecturer and writer. As a political activist his career concentrated upon Finsbury, whose radical–secularist axis was dominated by Spenceans. The First London Co-operative Manufacturing Society of which he writes so informatively in the *Life* (pp. 22–23) was one such Finsbury organisation. For it Davenport wrote his 'Co-operator's Catechism' (see below, pp. 81–92), an invaluable insight into grass-roots 'Owenism' and among the most important of his works for the historian. Davenport's description of Robert Owen's Labour Exchange is also highly interesting in the *Life*, but he passes over some other central aspects of his political career at this time. For example he was a founder member of a Finsbury group of freethinkers, co-operators, and Spenceans, which met at the Optimists', or Philadelphian, Chapel. His associates here included James Watson, and the shipbuilders' leader John Gast.[16] One of the most active and well-organised sections of the National Union of the Working Classes (NUWC) was located here, with Davenport a class leader. This section was in the vanguard of radical discussion in the capital, with Davenport typically forthright in his contributions to the unstamped press at this time: three items in the following further selection of his work are drawn from the *Poor Man's Guardian*, the focal point of the radical movement at this time.

It was the Finsbury section of the NUWC which, at the height of the Reform Bill crisis, petitioned the House of Commons to confiscate the landed estates of recalcitrant peers. It was Finsbury which furnished the majority of the committee of the Victim Fund, the organisation above all others which did most at this time to sustain the campaign for an unstamped press. Finally, it was Finsbury that dominated the NUWC sub-committee appointed to campaign for a national convention (though Davenport himself was not a member). This was the group which called the public meeting in May 1833 which culminated in the infamous Cold Bath Fields incident, in which two Metropolitan policemen were killed during the tumultuous dispersal of the crowd. At the ensuing inquest a controversial verdict of justifiable homicide was returned by the coroner's jury. 'The object of the Government,' claimed Davenport in a letter to the press, 'was not to warn but to surround and slaughter! It is clear to me, that this police mob, will, sooner or later, be the instruments of a revolution. It therefore behoves every friend of peace, order, and good government, to be on their guard against these common disturbers of peaceable society.'[17]

Davenport's attitude to the police at Cold Bath Fields further illustrates how his autobiography offers only a sanitised account of his political career. It is, though, the omission of any mention of Chartism which is most startling to the modern reader. In spite of advancing years and poor health, Allen Davenport was a far from passive supporter of the movement. As one of the founders of the East London Democratic Association (ELDA), and its first president, he occupied a central position in the earliest years of metropolitan Chartism. His article 'Universal Suffrage' (below pp. 100–101), published in Harney's militant physical force Chartist weekly *The London Democrat* indicates that Davenport's political views had not softened. The Democratic Association was the more revolutionary of the two organisations from which the movement grew in the capital, the other being the London Working Men's

Association: and of this, too, Davenport was a member. He was in addition elected to the executive of the Central National Association, a short-lived attempt (March–April 1837) at co-operation between London radicals. The Association also involved, through J. B. Bernard and the Cambridgeshire Farmers' Association, an element of home counties' participation not usually noticed in Chartism. At a local level Davenport was also a supporter of the City Charter, and Shoreditch Democratic Associations.[18]

Given the revolutionary nature of post-war Spenceanism it is perhaps understandable that Davenport should have chosen, even thirty years later, to obscure his part in it. That he should have passed-over aspects of his subsequent political career to concentrate upon co-operation and Owenism may be ascribed to a desire for balance within a work only partly devoted to politics; but the omission of any reference to Chartism presents a peculiar problem. Arguably it is this silence which is the autobiography's most notable, and paradoxically even informative, feature.

The implication is that by the mid-1840s Chartism no longer constituted a meaningful presence in metropolitan popular politics. After a lifetime committed to radicalism, and therefore all too-aware of its uneven progress, Davenport would seem to have viewed Chartism in 1845 as finished, and perhaps even as having had little long-term significance. As David Goodway, in his seminal work on London Chartism points out: 'After 1842 London Chartism drastically contracted; and until the revival of 1847–8 there were never more than some ten active localities.'[19] Comparatively few formal organisations within metropolitan radicalism lasted long. ELDA was itself dormant for several months in 1838; it reformed as the London Democratic Association in August of that year, but ultimately dwindled into a branch of the National Chartist Association in 1841. Davenport may well have regarded it as simply one among many of the often volatile organisations to which he had belonged in almost forty years of political activism. Only in retrospect and mindful of Chartism's resurgence in 1848, which was especially obvious in London, does the ELDA assume a lasting significance, merging as it did the energies of radicals whose experience extended as far back as the London Corresponding Society, with a younger generation.

Davenport's silence on the subject of Chartism is eloquent testimony to the slump in the movement's fortunes in the mid-1840s. However, had he chosen to detail his involvement the account might still implicitly have devalued the significance of the years 1836–40. Allen Davenport was among those Chartists whose response to the setbacks the movement experienced in 1839–40 led to the 'new move', the emphasis of which was upon education, class co-operation and peaceable politics. As much as this represented a rejection of the revolutionary principles of ELDA for

Davenport, it also expressed his continuing confidence in the political potential of class co-operation (which had also led him into the Central National Association), and his long-held belief in the centrality of education to the working-class cause. *The English Institutions* (below, pp. 102–10) is a poetic treatment of the central 'new move' issue of workers' education. As the autobiography explains (p. 26), whilst characteristically omitting to mention Chartism, Davenport was an early supporter of William Lovett's Holborn-based National Association. Yet at the same time Davenport combined his participation with vocal support for another venture, the Chartist Land Plan, which was led by the Chartist with whom Lovett is most often contrasted: Feargus O'Connor. In the months following the publication of the *Life* he was warm in his support of the Plan, eulogising Feargus O'Connor and chiding socialists for allowing the initiative in practical agrarian experiment to slip from them. 'The Land, the People's Farm', reproduced in this collection and virtually his last publication, was a poetic intervention in the revised debate on landed property.[20]

Why should a committed Spencean, for whom private property in land was anathema, endorse the Land Plan? As a political journalist Davenport's energies were firmly focused on the land question, sometimes to the exasperation of his colleagues. 'If I know anything of the general disposition of the readers of "The Republican",' Carlile once wrote to him, 'it is that they do not want *more last words* about "Agrarian Equality".'[21] Davenport had always been impatient to get involved in a practical 'back to the land' scheme. For example in 1839 he unsuccessfully applied to join an unofficial Owenite socialist community at Manea Fen, Cambridgeshire. Though turned-down because the community had sufficient shoemakers, he remained an enthusiastic advocate through the London branch of its supporters. His belief in the necessity of class co-operation was in part derived from the strength of his agrarian views. Following Spence in identifying the distribution of land as the key to economic and political injustice, Davenport inclined to view the middle classes as potential allies in the battle against an all-powerful landed interest. Furthermore, as a consequence of the rout of the 'ladies' men' in the strike of 1813, Davenport was imbued with a lasting scepticism as to the efficacy of trades combinations. Their main effect, he argued in 1825, was to produce nothing 'but discontent and misery'. Their every effort was undermined by surplus labour, and it was upon the elimination of the latter that Davenport concentrated his political energies. This was a central feature of the Chartist Land Plan, with its expressed objective of thinning, 'the artificial labour market by employing thousands now destitute, and constituting an idle reserve to enable capitalists to live and make fortunes upon the reduction of wages.' In this respect agrarian radicalism clearly lay at the cutting-edge of working-class consciousness; but it also drew heavily on an older radicalism, heir to the assumptions of the 'country party' of the eighteenth century, and identifying the machinations of the landed establishment as the one target above all that must be levelled. Because of its emphatic belief that the roots of social and economic injustice lay in the existing ownership of the land, agrarianism was inevitably bound-up with this deeply felt opposition to 'old corruption'. After a lifetime dedicated to the tenets of agrarian reform, it was thus not out of character for Davenport to endorse a scheme which appeared (whatever its shortcomings from a socialist point of view) to be able to undermine the monopoly of the land, 'the source of every social and political evil . . . every law which grinds the face of the poor'.[22]

Adult education

Davenport's commitment to Spenceanism is clear from the pages of his *Life and Literary Pursuits*, but it is by no means as emphatic as one might expect from reading his other work. Direct political homilies are rejected in favour of an accumulative argument on the need for, and benefits of, education. This is typical of nineteenth-century working-class autobiography. Virtually all such works, because of their very nature as accounts of those who had triumphed intellectually over sometimes overwhelming odds, centralise and emphasise the educational achievement of the author. Davenport's is no exception in this, stressing (p. 3) 'the almost impossibilities I must have had to overcome, in raising myself from such a depth of poverty and obscurity', whilst venturing to assert that, 'Most of the persons who I ever read or heard of, whose genius had raised them from obscurity to public notice, had something, more or less, of an education . . . [But] as far as I know, I stand alone. I never was in any school, for the purpose of instruction, in all my life.'

Such a claim introduces a near-fictional element into *The Life and Literary Pursuits*, but this need not detract from its value as a historical document. 'When a worker senses that his life is different . . . and sets out to describe it in order to bring out its special quality, we have a kind of creativity at work which is one step before the composing of a work of fiction which has the same or similar end, namely inducing in the worker a sense of the concrete nature of his life, instilling pride in it precisely for those qualities.'[23] Davenport perceived the essence of his achievement not so much in his radical-political career as in his educational progress (though ultimately of course the two cannot be separated). This becomes clearer if we examine the character of Davenport's education, and those educational organisations with which he became involved during his adult life.

There are very few points in the text where Davenport gives details about his actual experience of learning. The most informative is his recollection of how he learnt to read (p. 4) using printed songsheets. Information about how he learnt his trade is particularly sparse. Davenport underwent no recognised apprenticeship. It is a tribute to his innate abilities that having learnt shoemaking (one assumes but imperfectly) in the army he was nonetheless readily accepted among the highly skilled 'ladies men' of the capital after a few years spent in non-society shops.

Like many autodidacts Davenport was acutely grateful for the patronage of the educated. This is well-illustrated in his pride that his play *The Social Age* had been performed before Robert Owen, a man with whom in several respects he disagreed, for example in the article 'Property in danger', reproduced below. This deference to Owen may be contrasted to the slighting reference to James Watson, a close political colleague and friend, for thwarting his attempts to get his epic poem *Urania* into print. Davenport was vulnerable (reading the *Life* and the 'specimens in the department of polite literature' attached to it, one may feel *too* vulnerable), to middle-class patronage. In spite of his own considerable achievements as an autodidact, Davenport typically reveals an exaggerated deference towards those whom he regarded as highly educated.

Yet the details of his involvement in adult education reveal how much he operated outside of middle-class patronage. Davenport never assumed an active role in the Mechanics' Institute movement, with the exception of Gould Square (Finsbury), which as we shall see was somewhat different. Most of the educational initiatives in which he was involved were of a directly radical political nature, such as the Optimists' Chapel, Owen's Grays Inn Road Institute, the National Association and the Eastern Institution. The first of these evolved into a Society for Scientific, Useful and Literary Information, and its core group were also the founders of the radical Eastern Institution.

Two other groups which were not directly political are singled-out in the *Life and Literary Pursuits*: the Great Tower Street Mutual Instruction Society, of which Davenport was president from its inception (p. 26), and the Finsbury Mutual Instruction Society (p. 27). Unlike the contemporary Mechanics' Institutes, Mutual Instruction Societies have received relatively little interest from historians. Yet a well-informed source of 1840 states, 'There appears to be scarcely a small town in Great Britain which has not at least one, and most have several.' Educational data compiled as part of the 1851 Census bears this out. Mutual Instruction Societies eschewed the increasingly middle-class agenda and leadership of the Mechanics' Institutes, in favour of a more authentically autonomous 'self-help initiative. Probably the best known was the Leeds group which first commissioned the lectures that were later published as Samuel Smiles'

Self Help. It had met first in a garden shed, and then in a disused cholera hospital.[24]

The Great Tower Street Society had been set up on the initiative of John Robinson, a friend of the influential freethinker and popular educator Rowland Detrosier, in 1836:

> to promote the moral and intellectual improvement of its members, by means of essays, lectures, discussions, and conversations on all subjects. The subscription of 1s per quarter constitutes a member (subject to the approval of a majority of the members at any meeting night) and entitles the member to the use of a library consisting of 500 volumes.[25]

With sixty members this mutual instruction society was larger than most. The Finsbury Society, which met in a private house in Bunhill Row, was almost certainly smaller. Great Tower Street also boasted 'a considerable quantity of apparatus for chemistry, optics, galvanism, etc.' Classes were held in Latin, botany, mechanics, mathematics, arithmetic, grammar and 'discussion'. It was particularly discussion classes which disturbed middle-class educationalists,

> ever ready to talk on anything or everything, no matter whether the subject was comprehended or not . . . the impression left was, that these associations of youths, for the purposes of mutual improvement, were, on the whole, more pernicious than otherwise; generating a shallow self-conceit in the minds of the young persons composing them, and leading them to gabble away, with scarcely an idea in their heads, yet all the while satisfied that their shadowless words were full of meaning.[26]

However, participants' accounts offer a different perspective; for example, a Nottinghamshire artisan writing in 1847:

> We discourse upon any subject that first presents itself to our minds, at the commencement of the evening, – hence the subjects are multifarious, as history, both ancient and modern, social progress, natural history, geology, geography, etc. . . . Every subject is illustrated with chalk upon a black board, also the names of persons or places written-up, which the pupils are made to repeat aloud, and after an hour's conversation, they are questioned as to the subject they have been discussing.[27]

Although Davenport included an elegy to the prime mover of the London Mechanics' Institute, George Birkbeck in his poem *The English Institutions*, it is clear that his personal energies in the educational field were focused on Mutual Instruction Societies and their like. The Mechanics' Institute of which he was president, Gould Square in Finsbury, was effectively a confederation of several Mutual Instruction Societies, pooling their resources to obtain outside speakers and run classes in less popular subjects. The significance of Mutual Instruction Societies lay less in their curriculum than in the democratic control of the organisation, and the fact that tutors were drawn from the members' own ranks and class. They were also more likely to open their doors on Sundays, and less likely to discourage the discussion of the twin bug-bears of the Mechanics' Institutes movement, politics and controversial theology.

Though a de-centralised initiative, these autonomous self-help educational groups were part of an enormous ground-swell of interest in learning. Their autonomy was part of their very power and Davenport, though as we have seen a supporter of class co-operation in politics, nevertheless believed in the need for a genuinely popular education if his dreams of social and political equality for all were to be realised. In Davenport's view even the much maligned, 'infant schools, though taught by village dames, /Are sources of the tributary streams.'[28]

Davenport's emphatic belief in the need for, and power of, popular education was typically Spencean. Like Spence before him, Davenport combined a powerful perception of the roots of economic inequality, lying in the land, with a vision of a new order to be achieved through the widest possible participation in education; and like other members of Spence's circle, his interest in adult education grew as the likelihood of their ever fomenting a radical *coup d'état* receded. Almost the last public appearance of the leader of the Spenceans after their founder's death, Thomas Evans, was on the platform at the inaugural meeting of the London Mechanics' Institute. In the autobiography Davenport mentions two other Spenceans, Jennison and Neesom, who were his associates in working-class adult education. In this they can be seen as reaffirming Thomas Spence's passionate belief that the growth of 'Reason, aided by the Art of Printing', was all that was needed to secure lasting radical reform.[29]

However, though an increasingly literate movement, much of the ideology of radicalism was transmitted not through writing or journalism but through the platforms at countless meetings, societies, and institutes. When the young George Julian Harney addressed an audience of Kent Chartists in 1845 and told them, 'his creed was – and Thomas Spence had taught it him – that "the Land is the people's farm", and that it belongs to the entire nation, not to individuals or classes', the lesson he cited, and the quote he gave, came from Spence via Davenport.[30] In the absence of any reprinting of Spence's work after his death in 1814, the transmission of his ideas through the networks which the Spenceans made was crucial. As a writer, lecturer, and educator Davenport played a central role here: he did so perhaps not 'almost single-handedly' as has been suggested.[31] Besides Davenport, Neesom and Jennison, the Spenceans John George, Edward Blandford, Samuel Waddington, James Mee and Thomas Preston all survived to become active Chartists. Davenport however was undoubtedly the most important of those Spenceans who survived their leader to place his ideas before new generations of radicals.

Davenport was thus an important vector for radical ideology across several generations of radicals. Indeed his contribution in this manner extended beyond his death. At the end of the nineteenth century both the English Land Nationalisation Society and the Independent Labour Party published accounts of Spence's life and work which drew extensively on Davenport's *Life, Writings, and Principles of Thomas Spence*. The English Land Nationalisation Society also reprinted Davenport's 'Elegy on the Author of the Spencean System'. Alone of his followers, Davenport's name was coupled with that of Spence himself on the Reformers' Memorial erected in Kensal Green Cemetery in 1885.[32]

Conclusion

The Life and Literary Pursuits of Allen Davenport . . . written by himself is by no means as arbitrary in its selection of material as it first seems. The care with which it is constructed underlines that working-class autobiography is never artless. It is valuable for its contemporary view of metropolitan radicalism and adult education, and for the incidental information it makes available about the career of a significant working-class politician and educator. Of course Davenport was not a Francis Place, nor a John Gast: but the significance of individual figures like them is almost habitually exaggerated. The momentum of the labour movement was derived principally from the most significant part of its leadership, that part which was drawn from the ranks of the working class and which remained there. Histories of labour which are cast largely in terms of leaders and followers, of faceless ideologies, or equally faceless aggregates of workers, miss the detail of daily economic, educational and political struggle, and with it the contribution of those like Davenport, the numbers unlimited whose talents, energies and fortitude constituted the spine of radical leadership. Most have no memorial, but Allen Davenport's prolific output as a political journalist, culminating in this autobiography, offers an insight to the 'grass-roots' of the nineteenth-century working-class movement.

However, it would be naïve to suppose that the value of Davenport's *Life and Literary Pursuits* subsists solely at the level of factual information about the various movements of which he was part. The foregoing analysis has placed much emphasis upon the 'silences' of the autobiography. This has not been done simply with the intention of rounding-out the author's self-portrait. It would be ridiculous to expect any autobiography not to be silent on some aspects of its subject/author's life, since any retrospective narrative form is inevitably selective. It is the nature and purpose of the selection process which demands critical attention. The act of writing an autobiography is a conscious recognition that in some critical aspects the subject's life is *not* at one with the short and simple annals of the poor (to adapt Davenport's introductory reference to Gray's *Elegy*). Some silences are of a relatively low-order of importance: Davenport offers little information about the work process within shoemaking, indeed ignoring the trade completely except where it intersected with his political career through trade unionism. Other silences are more complicated. What should we make of the failure ever to mention his daughter? Was their relationship a painful one? Had she, in either dying, marrying or moving away, removed herself from her father's active consciousness? Or was such a removal something of which Davenport was painfully conscious, and therefore unwilling to contemplate – even fleetingly – in the public arena of the *Life*? The failure even to acknowledge the existence of his child is especially striking given the warmth with which the biography refers to its author's marriage. Yet even here Davenport never mentions his wife by name.

The disregard of family details is less puzzling if we view *The Life and Literary Pursuits of Allen Davenport* as essentially a statement about a literary and political career to which domestic circumstances had been strictly subordinate. As both his title and introduction suggest, Davenport was at pains to stake a claim for a literary reputation. Some substantial later writing is ignored whilst, for example, his collection of poems *The Muse's Wreath* is referred to at some length, with revealing exaggeration as to the reception it received (see p. 22 and note). There is a tension here, however, since so much of Davenport's literary output – and virtually all that part of it on which his contemporary reputation rested – was highly politicised. The last three paragraphs of this autobiography (pp. 27–9) are the key to its author's purpose in writing, and therefore to the selection of material. They form a suddenly passionate statement of the way in which political and educational progress are intertwined, and of how the intellectual progress of the working class reinforces the claim for 'an universal change in the political and social system of nations'. In it Davenport blends elements of Spencean, early socialist and 'New Move' Chartist rhetoric. His implied readership is emphatically clear: on the one hand 'his own order, who might happen to be placed at a still greater distance from the wholesome and cheering rays of that bright intellectual sun, which has now arrived at such an imposing altitude'; and on the other those in a position to effect a change in the direction of government policy. Earlier it was suggested that the autobiography's indifference to Chartism was indicative of Davenport regarding the life of the movement as ended. However, it is obvious that whatever doubts Davenport held about the likely future capacity of Chartism to effect change, as a socialist he typically still expected 'the approaching storm – the moral earthquake, which will shake the world, and convulse Europe from its centre to its circumference'. This vision of an imminent, secularised millennium, and the language in which it is cast, is typical of early English socialism.

However, Davenport would appear to have remained, sufficiently pragmatic a politician to realise that suppression of certain aspects of his political career might better serve the fulfilment of his vision. He does not fudge the need for 'a more equal distribution of human subsistence', which had been a consistent belief ever since his conversion to Spenceanism. However, his sanitised account of post-war radicalism and the part he had played in it was consciously intended to attract the approval not only of a middle-class readership, but also of those many working-class radicals whose 'march of mind' was towards respectability. It is almost a platitude to observe that the radical politics of 1845 were not those of 1819; neither were they those of 1839. Writing an autobiography was a means by which Allen Davenport could come to terms with the changing political and cultural contexts of his last years. Consciously or subconsciously the act of writing his *Life* may thus have functioned as a means of 'cultural bonding' for its author, which he used both to integrate himself within the changing radicalism of the mid-1840s, and to continue to understand what was going on around him.[33]

Notes

1 *The Reasoner* II, 29 (January 1847) p. 18; *N[orthern] S[tar]* 17 October 1846.
2 *NS* 30 August 1845.
3 *NS* 3, 17 and 24 October, 7 November, 5 December 1846; *The Reasoner* I, 18 (30 September) p. 245, 20 (14 October) p. 264 and 21 (21 October 1846) p. 271.
4 There are reports of the funeral in *The Reasoner* II p. 18, and *The Utilitarian Record* II p. 1, 4–5. Holyoake's memorial discourse was reprinted in his *Life and Character of Richard Carlile* (1849) pp. 29–31.
5 *NS* 4 March 1843.
6 See the reports in *NS* and *The Reasoner* cited above, also Holyoake's *Letterbook* in the Bishopsgate Institute, London.
7 Vincent (1977) p. x.
8 *Co-operative Magazine* 10 and 11 (October–November 1826).
9 *The News* 476 (28 August) and 479 (18 September 1814); *Diligent Observer* I, 4 (23 August 1817).
10 The Spencean underground is analysed in Chase (1988) pp. 78–120, and McCalman (1988) pp. 7–151.
11 Public Record Office (Kew) H[ome] O[ffice] 42/197, 18 October 1819 – report of constables Plush and Matthewson.
12 HO 42/191, 10 August 1819 – report of Chetwade.
13 HO 42/197, 18 October 1819 – report of Plush and Matthewson. For the

testimony of other shoemakers involved in Cato Street see: P. Benton, *History of Rochford Hundred* (Rochford, 1867), p. 343; A Master Shoemaker, 'My Life and Adventures', *Boot and Shoemaker* 14 June–9 August 1879; and John Brown, *Sixty Years' Gleanings From Life's Harvest* (Cambridge, 1858), p. 278. See also Mansfield (1979) and Chase (1988) pp. 117–20.

14 *Penny Papers for the People* 27 May 1831; *Sherwin's Weekly Political Register* 13 June 1818.

15 *Republican* 20 June 1823; 25 August 1826; *Cosmopolite* 22 September 1832, 9 March 1833.

16 For Gast see Prothero (1979).

17 *Working Man's Friend and Political Instructor* 24 (1 June 1833). On the Cold Bath Fields incident see Chase (1988), pp. 161–2 and Thurston (1967).

18 Davenport's main Chartist statement was an article, 'Universal Suffrage', in the *London Democrat* 9 (8 June 1839). For his contribution to the movement see especially *London Mercury* 18 June 1837; *London Dispatch* 4 June 1837, 11 February 1838; and *Northern Star*, 21 November 1840; Thompson, 1971, pp. 55–6, reprints the inaugural address of the East London Democratic Association to which Davenport was a signatory. On the Association and its successor the LDA, see Bennett (1982) pp. 87–119.

19 Goodway (1982a) p. 54.

20 It is unclear how active Davenport was in the National Association, but see the *National Association Gazette* 13 (26 March) and 14 (2 April 1842). His notable statements on the Land Plan are to be found in *Northern Star*, 29 August 1846, and the *Reasoner* vol. 1, 10, (6 August 1846), pp. 157–8.

21 *Republican* 25 January 1825.

22 *Trades' Newspaper and Mechanics' Weekly Journal* 21 (4 December 1825), p. 322; *NS* 22 March 1845, 12 August 1848. For a detailed analysis of radical agrarianism see Chase (1988).

23 Goldstein (1984) p. 339; cf John Harrison's observation: 'In fact, the autobiography is an art form, closely akin to the novel', *Times Literary Supplement* 11–17 September 1987, p. 992. There is of course a sizeable secondary literature on autobiography as a literary genre: see particularly Fleishman (1983), Olney (1988), Pascal (1960) and Sturrock (1993); and on working-class autobiography Vincent (1981) and Gagnier (1987).

24 *London Saturday Journal* 11 April 1840; Samuel Smiles, *Self Help* (1860; New Edition, 1873) pp. vii–ix. On Mutual Instruction Societies see Harrison (1961) passim; Kirk (1985), pp. 197–8, and 208–14; Radcliffe (1986) pp. 1–16; Green (1990), pp. 25–43.

25 *London Saturday Journal* 29 February 1840. On Detrosier see Williams (1965).

26 *London Saturday Journal* 29 February 1840.

27 Christopher Thompson, *The Autobiography of an Artisan* (Nottingham, 1847), p. 335.

28 *English Institutions* (1842) p. 109 (below).

29 Quotations from Thomas Spence, *The Important Trial of Thomas Spence for a Political Pamphlet Entitled 'The Restorer of Society to its Natural State'* (2nd edition, 1807) p. 35. On Spenceanism and education see Chase (1988).

30 *NS* 30 August 1845. For Davenport's influence on Harney see also Schoyen (1958) pp. 5, 12, 14, 28, 147; and Gregory Claeys (1989) pp. 240–41.

31 Claeys (1987) pp. 157–9, 216.

32 Frederick Verinder, *Land for the Landless* (English Land Restoration League,

1896); J.M. Davidson, *Concerning Four Precursors of Henry George and the Single Tax* (Labour Leader, Glasgow, 1900). The Reformers' Memorial still stands: for its historical background see the entry on Anne Isabella [Lady] Byron in J. Bellamy and J. Saville (eds), *Dictionary of Labour Biography, vol.* 2 (1974) pp. 77–8.

33 On autobiography and 'cultural bonding' see Sturrock (1993), pp. 289–91.

A Further Selection from the Works of Allen Davenport

Davenport added selections of his work to both the *Life* and *The English Institutions*. Those accompanying the autobiography are reprinted above with the original text as the author intended. In the following compilation *The English Institutions* is included, along with the additional material intended by the author: 'Pictoria; or the Origin of Painting'; 'The King of the Barricades'; 'The Midnight Dream' (accompanied by a dedicatory note to Thomas Cooper); and 'The Showman'.

Twelve further works selected by the editor have been added, and the whole sequence placed in chronological order, to give a genuinely representative selection of Davenport's poetry and political journalism across the four decades of his career as a writer.

'The Devil Out-Devilled', from *Sherwin's Weekly Political Register*, 29 August 1818.

It has long been asserted the old one, the DEVIL,
Is the father of vice, and the cause of all evil;
But I'll make it appear to both wicked and sainted,
There are men still more black than the DEVIL is painted.

The devil, NAPOLEON, once haunted our shore,
He's banished, and now we're worse off than before;
For thousand's of DEVILS sprang up in his stead,
From the tail of the Nation, right up to its head;

There are DEVILS in every rank of the state,
All ages, all sizes, both little and great; –
At COURT, – in the SENATE, – and if you will search,
Very many there are to be found in the CHURCH!

There are devil informers, each a devilish spy,
And some that sell boroughs, and others that buy,
Some feed on large pensions they do not deserve,
While other poor devils are ready to starve! –

There are DEVILS trained up in all parts of the Nation,
Then sent up to town to perform legislation;
Where sessions are held in that great PANDEMONIUM*,
Where every last action receives an "encomium".

For SATAN himself never gained more applause,
Then that ruffian set who suspended our laws;
Though the world he betrayed, as in record we find,
'Twas left to these DEVILS to torture mankind;

Who INNOCENCE punish, then pass a decree,
To indemnify DEVILS, and let them go free,
Then rail not against SATAN, the champion of evil,
The base BOROUGH-MONGERS have out-done the DEVIL!

A.D.

*House of Borough-mongers

From *Sherwin's Weekly Political Register* 19 September 1818

TO THE EDITOR OF THE POLITICAL REGISTER.

SIR,

In the last letter I addressed you I endeavoured to defend the working classes against their idle and insolent oppressors; or figuratively speaking, to defend the active and industrious bees, against the indolent and worthless drones that disgrace the great hive of society. In the present letter I will endeavour to point out the extreme ignorance of the borough-mongers in the choice of the means they make use of, in order to defend their plunder, and to arrest that crisis, which no human hand will be able to prevent. It is not necessary for me to explain in what manner the little bees dispose of their drones; it will be sufficient to say, that if they find them guilty of idleness, or robbery, they put them to death without any ceremony; and the reason why our tyrants tremble when they see a crowd, and entrench themselves behind phalanxes of mercenary bayonets is, the consciousness that their conduct justifies the revolt of the People; and that they consequently deserve death at the hand of every free-man. So powerfully does fear operate on their minds, that they betray their alarm at the most trifling circumstance; no sooner do they receive information that the People are about to assemble, no matter for what purpose, but they order their soldiers under arms, construct moveable batteries, load the cannon, and make every preparation, the same as if the whole metropolis was about to be taken by storm. In the mean time the whole hireling press is put in request to cheer up another portion of the People by telling them that they have nothing to fear, since they have a vigilant magistracy, active subordinates, and a loyal soldiery! Mark this, a loyal soldiery! Well may Mr. Hunt hold this up to ridicule in Palace Yard. Oh, the blabbing fools, this was making a plain confession that loyalty is only to be found with the soldiers and the borough-mongers. But this was not all, previous to the meeting in Palace Yard, and indeed previous to every meeting of the People, the Editor of the "*News*" makes it his business to persuade the People not to assemble together on any account, for that it is very probable that Mr. Hunt, or some of his connections, holds communications with the Government, and if that should not be the case, the Government will be sure to send spies and informers to the meetings, in order to stir up rioting, and thereby prevent reform instead of hastening it. Thus does this overwise editor aid the Government with all the means in his power, by trying to make the People have the same dread of spies and informers, as the children of our forefathers had of ghosts and goblins. D——n the spies and informers, I was going to say; I do not know any body that cares any thing about them, save this sage editor, but he I suppose quiets his children by telling them that Oliver or Castles are Canning! Thousands of the People, however, in spite of all these newspaper denunciations, and all the military preparations described above, repaired to Palace Yard, and there dispassionately discussed, and unanimously passed a Remonstrance to the Prince Regent, and then with the greatest good-nature (in imitation of our brave soldiers and sailors before they engage a foreign foe) gave three hearty cheers, and marched off, with their brave champion at their head, with the greatest regularity to the Secretary of State's office, there deposited their Remonstrance to the Regent, and then retired in the best possible order to their respective homes. Probably the Editor of the *News* may call all those People spies and informers, for they certainly went to see and hear all that they could, and when they had so done, they themselves went to Lord Sidmouth, and delivered a written account of their object into the hand of his Lordship to convey to our most gracious Prince Regent. But to return to the vigilant magistracy, and the loyal soldiery, though it is not on the magistracy that the borough-mongers and their tools depend; oh, no! it is on the army, and the paper money, that their whole system depends; short sighted and forgetful mortals! Have they then forgot that the French army (and a braver army never existed) shouted "*vive le Roi*" and "*vive Napoleon*" in the same breath! and perhaps in less than two years time will shout "*vive la republique:*" have they forgot, too, how much they praised that part of the Saxon army who violated their oaths, deserted their King, and in the same moment discharged their cannon upon their own countrymen? And why might not what have happened, happen again? And are they so blind that they cannot perceive that the People have it in their power to destroy the paper bubble whenever they choose? "Ah!" exclaim the borough-tyrants, "but a French army and an English army are quite different things, the French were never much to be depended upon, having too much levity in their manners; but the English army, having a deeper sense of moral obligations, there can be no fear that they will violate the oath of their engagement to defend their King and country:" indeed! why they, in conjunction with the tyrants who direct their movements, have already violated the oath of their engagements, by enslaving their King, by cutting off all communication with his subjects, and thereby making him answerable for acts of injustice and oppression, that had he received the warning and prayers of his faithful and loyal People, he would not only not have committed himself, but he would not have suffered those around to have done so. Thus, then, instead of defending their Sovereign, they have placed him under circumstances in a parallel with those of Charles I. and Louis XVI. So much for serving and defending their King! Now let us see how the tyrants aided by their army have served and defended their country, and in doing this, we need only look over the history of their transactions since the French revolution, for during that period every species of fraud, perfidy, treachery, rapine, murder, and in short almost all the ills, from which our reverend divines and all the good People in the churches do continually cry, "good Lord deliver us." The result of which is that they have made famine to exist amidst plenty; they caused plagues to rage amongst the population through the want of common necessaries to feed and clothe the People, they have reduced the greatest part of the labouring classes to a starving state, and though their sufferings are become past endurance, to murmur is sedition,—to complain is treason, and should they dare to raise their voice against their cruel oppressors, the State ruffians without much ceremony order their "loyal soldiery" to fire vollies of musketry into the unarmed populace; so musical to their ears are the terrible sounds of killed and wounded; so hardened are their hearts that they can gaze with savage joy on the mangled dead, and hear with transport the agonizing groans of the dying victims! oh! ye brave and enlightened mechanics of Manchester will you ever forget your murdering tyrants?—your human butchers? We have not yet forgot our Piccadilly butchers, although they have been to Waterloo to retrieve their honour. But still Sir, I would wish to think as favourably of the soldiers as possible, because I believe when most of them entered the service things were called by their own names, therefore they were sworn in to one thing and had to practice another. The form of their oath should have run thus: 'will you fight against liberty in every part of the world wherever you should happen to be sent, against every free Government and against every free People, and after you have enslaved Europe—plundered and murdered the Indians,—after you have restored Louis the Desired, Ferdinand the Beloved, the Pope, and the Inquisition!—And if in doing all these things your country should become so much burthened with heavy taxes, so as to cause commerce to diminish, and all kinds of trade to be slack, or should the wages of the mechanics and labourers be so low that hunger may compel them to ask for more, will you then turn your arms against your starving countrymen, and imbrue your hands, if it should so happen, in the blood of your aged parents, of your blooming sisters, or even in the blood of those nearer and dearer than all, your affectionate wives, or your innocent and helpless children? A portion, or the whole of this may happen when you fire into large crowds of the People. Will you do all these things in order to protect a borough-mongering system, a corrupted House of Commons, a company of swindlers, commonly called Directors, and finally assist to establish a complete military despotism, and to place the lives and fortunes of all the inhabitants of the British empire, at the disposal of a cruel and blood-thirsty oligarchy, whose will alone shall be the law?' Had the above interrogatories been put to each soldier as he entered the service, and then had each soldier answered in the affirmative by kissing the bible, he would then have been sworn in consistently with the duties he had, and may have to perform. The error which has caused those destructive convulsions that have demoralized in a great measure the world, originated with the borough- ruffians themselves; they first swore that wrong was right, and then commanded the army to make their assertion good by bayonetting all those who should any way oppose it; and the People of England were compelled to part with their money, and in some instances, with their furniture and clothes; in order to pay their tyrants for swearing wrong was right—the soldiers for endeavouring to make the People believe it by thrusting it down their throats with the point of the sword, and to bribe the Governments of foreign Nations to act upon the same principles in their own dominions; and to unite with the borough-mongers to destroy both the rights and the liberties of mankind, by setting up an European oligarchy, which holds by usurpation the power of buying, selling, and bartering away the bodies and souls of two hundred millions of human beings! Now, Sir, these coercive measures with all their concomitants, which have, for thirty years, afflicted the world, have been carried on principally to prevent one grand object, namely, "a radical reform" in the English House of Commons; and here, the ignorance as well as the wickedness of the borough-mongers and their vile tools, is conspicuous, for the very means they have employed to prevent have hastened that event, which in spite of all the military force in Europe,—in spite of all the sapient magistrates and corrupted judges,—in spite of chains and dungeons, axes, and gibbets, must, and will very soon take place. Thus do tyrants always strike at random, while justice with an unerring hand never misses her mark. They begin to feel all the horrors of their approaching fate, and like drowning men grasp at straws. Witness their weak and futile attempts to inundate the country with Saving Banks and Bible Associations;—attempts which if successful would defeat the very purpose for which they are intended. With respect to the "Banks for Savings," let us suppose them for a moment to be seconded by the People, let us suppose that the sober and industrious were to become believers in their utility, what would be the immediate consequence? They would lay down their savings, their little long-hoarded sums, on the strength of this sham security, and supposing all the parties concerned to act according to the professions of the projectors of the institution their savings would be safe as long as the *funding system* would be safe. But who knows how long that system would continue to wear its present appearance of security? Who that knows its baseless condition, its liability to be swept off at any moment whenever the breeze of public opinion shall veer to a different quarter of the political compass,—who is it then that views "things as they are," that would place his hopes on so precarious a security? *Public credit*, it has been very justly observed is no more than "*suspicion asleep*," and the moment suspicion becomes awake, public credit dies away as a natural consequence. Whenever this great event takes place, what will be the feelings of the People,—the poor and industrious whose *little* ALL has been deposited in that mock system of security—the *funding system*. How will the People feel to those who have *seduced* them by every species of temptation, who have entrapped them by lures the most artful, who have betrayed them by the violation of promises the most faithful?

As for Bible Societies, whatever may be the intentions of their founders, their direct tendency is to teach rebellion and resistance to the People. There is no book in the English language, which, if properly understood, is more diametrically opposed to the present order of things than the Bible. The Clergy must be *mad* to promote the circulation of such a book. Its doctrine is in every respect the reverse of monarchy and its universal circulation will inevitably do away with priestcraft.

It is therefore evident that the two schemes which I have noticed can have but one tendency,—which is, the ruin and destruction of the accursed borough-mongering system. Whatever our oppressors may think on the subject, the day of retribution must inevitably come, and their schemes, instead of putting it off, will only hasten its arrival. What then will be their destiny when the awful day of reckoning shall arrive? will they fly,—a fallen tyrant's last resource? Oh no, they would find an enemy at every step, armed with sword of retributive justice. Will they stoop to apologize, and throw themselves on the mercy of the People? No, no, they have committed such crimes against the People, that it would be a crime in the People to pardon them. What ought to be their doom? Let the shades of Cashman, Brandreth, Ludlam and Turner, answer the question!

Editor's note: Cashman was an Irish sailor hanged for his part in the Spa Fields Riot of 1816; Brandreth, Ludlam and Turner were hanged for their part in the Pentridge Rising of 1817.

The Kings;
or
Legitamacy Unmasked (1819)

T. Pray tell me friend, for you can tell such things,
From whom descended all the race of Kings;
What gave them birth, what were their origin?

D. They sprung from ruffian-force, and venal sin;
And few have reign'd who have not been a scourge,
From mighty Nimrod down to the fourth George!
Their tyranny with their succession run,
From age to age, from father to the son;
Train'd up to conquest, is the royal boy,
And taught the glorious science to destroy;
Instructed how to copy former knaves,
And treat his people like a herd of slaves;
To wage unjust and sanguinary wars,
Till half mankind are mark'd with wounds and scars.
To waste the people's treasure, and their blood,
Gives princes joy, for evil is their good;
Such are the boons the Lord's anointed brings
Such are the blessings we derive from kings!

T. Hush traitorous wight, nor date that theme prolong,
Since all allow, "the king can do no wrong;"
You are too warm, you lose your temper quite,
Though ministers do wrong kings may be right.

D. What e'er is once transacted in my name,
Becomes my act, though it should cause me shame;
Till contradiction sets the matter right,
And makes the conscious villain shun my sight:—
Then tell me not, a king can harmless be,
Amidst a base corrupted ministry;
If he look on, and does not check their sway.
Is he, or is he not, more vile than they?

T. I see you have abilities for satire,
But pray be careful how you treat this matter;
Rail where you will, men will revere the station
Of the chief man, APPOINTED BY THE NATION;
Such arguments will be consider'd bad,
Though poets rave, they should not run stark mad,
Kings oft are blam'd for what they never do,—

D. So are their slaves, and often punish'd too!
Oft left to starve, yet if they ask for bread,

They oft receive an halter in its stead,
From those who in infernal league combined,
In peace or war to fleece and starve mankind;
Who make the nations groan beneath their sway,
Then hire knaves, the people to betray;
Such are the plans of kingly government,
Thus kings attempt to cure all discontent.—

T. If there be such, what ought to be their doom?

D. Ask Brutus, Ravellac and Ankerstroom.
He who refuse to hear a nation's cries,
What man would mourn, if such a tyrant dies?
So hardened are the sons of royalty,
'Tis treason but to wish for liberty;
They govern nations with an iron rod,
Oppress the people, and blaspheme their God!

T. I own bad rulers some great states enthral,
But your wide censure strikes at one and all:
Have there been none then that deserve our praise,
From good old Alfred down to George's days?

D. Not one, that I have ever understood
Who has not done more mischief far than good.
To royalty the world owes half its crimes,
Down from the deluge to the present times;
Scarce was the flood commanded to subside,
When royalty burst forth with all its pride.
With hunting, Nimrod, monarchy began,
But his successors have improv'd the plan;
The former sought his victims in the chase,
The latter preys upon the human race:
For this proud Ninus mounted on his car,
And taught the trade of battle, and of war,
Then rush'd through Asia like a second flood,
And steep'd her fertile plains in human blood.
So did Sesostris, the same work pursue,
And strove his predecessor to out do;
Pushing his conquest over sea, and land,
Till millions fell beneath his iron hand;
Before his march each hill and valley smil'd,
At his command, whole states became a wild.
And Alexander too, old Philip's son,
To finish what his father had begun,
The flag of universal war unfurl'd,
And too successful bore it through the world:
To gain the name of universal Lord,
He lay'd the nations waste with fire and sword,
From the Marmora to the Indian shore,
Then wept because he could destroy no more:—
Intoxicated with his own success,
He sunk beneath the man in wild excess,

Or mimic'd on his throne the thunderer's nod,
Call'd Ammon father, and assumed the God.

T. What monarchs were two thousand years ago,
Bears no resemblance to what they are now.

D. True. Ancient kings as I've already shewn,
Robb'd foreign states, the modern rob their own.
If kings in former times were idoliz'd,
Our modern kings, are more to be despis'd,
Who play the tyrant;—yet affect the sage,
Act the imposter, and disgrace the age;
Who to keep up their tyranny and fraud,
Pretend to have a right deriv'd from God.

T. Yet, if by pretences kings blaspheme,
Do not their subjects do the very same?
For there are men, although it may seem odd,
That kneel to kings, who never knelt to God.
Nor is the love of kings confined to man,
Even insects act upon the self same plan;
Bees have their king, who act by nature's laws,
To whom they yield obedience, and applause,
With loyalty as firm, as pure their love,
As that of angels to the king above.
Touch but their monarch, and you'll have to strive,
With the whole population of the hive.

D. And should you do one humming subject harm,
Should not you be assail'd by all the swarm?—
Then is the hive a commonwealth complete,
Blest with the sweets of a republic state;
Perhaps the master bee is, after all,
An humble president,— no king at all.

T. That chief, whose soul, on mankind's good is bent,
Whether Emperor, or King, or President;
And who to guilt alone extends the rod,
Is the true representative of God.

D. But he whose reign is one continued evil,
Was surely sent to represent the Devil;
And such there are, and one whom I could name,
Who virtue scorns, and triumphs in his shame;
Who lends his sanction to the worst of knaves,
To rule Freemen, by laws decreed for slaves.

T. 'Tis by our license when a tyrant rules,
Where kings are knaves, are not the people fools?
A Prince's duty is to govern well,
If not, the people's right is to expel;
If both neglect it then remains for you,
To show which is most guilty of the two.
Suppose a man in any commonwealth,
Were to procure a crown, and crown himself,—

Suppose the people on the other hand,
Reject his claim, and laugh at his command;
He'd be no more a king by his own law,
Than would a madman with his crown of straw;
The madman would a tear from pity call,
The fool would be the laughing stock of all;
And be compelled to lay his crown aside,
And seek a place, his empty head to hide.

D. The people have it in their pow'r I own,
Either to set up kings, or put them down;
Then should not kings bestow some little care,
On those to whom they owe the crown they wear?—
Yet show me one of all the kingly brood,
That is not stain'd with base ingratitude!
Those people who delight in royal things,
I pity from my heart, let them have kings,
When Kish, the Hebrew, did his asses lose,
Saul sought, and found them in the foolish Jews,
Or what amounted to the self same thing,
They chose the Jackass-driver for the King;
Who while his subjects testified their joy,
Receiv'd the scepture only to destroy;
To spoil mankind, he made an holy cause,
And him that slaughter'd most gain'd most applause!
E'en Jesse's son, who bow'd before the Lord,
Learnt all the magic power of the sword;
And though some virtues in his actions shone,
His vices would have shook a Tarquin's throne:
For though this prince was after God's own heart,
He sometimes would perform the devil's part;
And much abus'd that pow'r which God had given,
Or else injustice does descend from heaven!
And his successor, who prolong'd his line,
Rul'd Israel too with the same right divine;
He ask'd for wisdom to direct his reign,
And just obtain'd enough to make him vain;
He built pavilions,— palaces, and grots,
Seraglios, pagod's, and splendid cots:
Imported luxuries from ev'ry clime,
Like some European kings, in our time;—
Maintain'd in grandeur from the people's stores,
Wives seven hundred, and three hundred w—s!—

T. Forbear rash man, those sacred writings spare,
What heaven imparted, shall not man revere?
That glorious guide to ages that are gone,
And still grows brighter as the time runs on;
That book of truth,— inimitable plan,
Dictated by a God, though wrote by man;
The greatest gift that Heaven ever gave,
It binds the broken heart, and frees the slave;

The lasting records of a Saviour's love,
And reconcilement of a God above!
Whoever makes attack on holy writ,
Will be despis'd however bright his wit.

D. I much revere the doctrine you proclaim,
But gentle friend you much mistake my aim,
My shafts are levell'd at no holy things,
My arrows only point at tyrant kings.
Belshazzar's sire, for trampling on the laws,
Became a beast, arm'd with a monster's claws;
Made the companion of the ox, and ass,
Drove to the field and doom'd to feed on grass;
Condemn'd like Lucifer to lick the dust,
By man despised, and by all Heaven accurst.
And Pharoh too, despising God's command,
Dealt out oppression with unsparing hand,
Till angry heaven with an out stretch'd arm,
Sent ev'ry plague which could the world alarm;
And smote the monarch for his proud disdain,
—His slaves for letting such a tyrant reign;
But harden'd still omnipotence he braves,
'Till crush'd beneath the heaven-commanded waves!

T. Mankind are different, in each different clime,
And all things change with course and lapse of time.

D. Not strictly so, you take too wide a range,
The laws of God, and Nature never change;
And truth, and justice and an honest fame,
Through ev'ry change will still remain the same.
Though kings proclaim, their right is from the Lord,
They wisely seek protection in the sword;–
Take but the king's protecting sword away,
And all their heavenly right will soon decay;
The people's will is every monarch's all,
Take but that prop away, and down they fall:—
If justice strike will heaven avert the blow?
The shades of Charles, and Louis answers, "No"!
In vain to Heaven they rais'd their royal hands,
In vain they call'd for aid to distant lands,
'Twas then too late and heaven reject'd their call,
The world combin'd, could not prevent their fall!
May every cruel despot share their fate,
May every tyrant's fall be as complete.

T. With you to overthrow all regal power?
Then may I never live to see the hour:—
I'd rather see things even, "as they are",
Then see my country bleed in civil war!
I cannot like the doctrine you advance,
Till I forget the massacres in France;
Till I forget those crimes which Gallia stain'd,

When Robespierre, Murat, and terror reign'd;
No sooner was one bloody tyrant dead,
Than twenty monsters sprung up in his stead;
Alternate factions exercis'd their sway,
And murder was, "the order of the day".
Nought could be heard but agonizing screams,
Nor seen, save towns, and villages in flames;
There brothers against brothers were array'd
Sons slew they wives, and friends their friends betray'd.

D. So have I seen a steed in winter pen'd,
Till grown familiar as an humble friend;
But when arriv'd the season to be free,
'He gallop'd, leap'd, and snort with furious glee,
Stop'd short then wheel'd,—some other beast enthral,
Or kick'd the poor companion of his stall;
Who had he never lost his liberty,
Would have been gentle though he had been free.
Where tyrants govern not one single good,
Can to the people flow, unstain'd with blood;
Had Louis yielded to a state reform,
France ne'er had witness'd such a frightful storm:
A storm that shook the world from pole to pole,
A storm that heaven itself could scarce controul!

T. But since that storm is spent, which gave such pain,
You wish not sure to stir it up again.

D. I wish to do away all royal pride,
And I've God's servant Joshua on my side,
That foe to kings,—that great heroic Jew,
Who more than thirty reigning princes slew,
Was Joshua for those regicides abhor'd?—
No,— prais'd by men, and sanction'd by the Lord!
And had Napoleon Joshua's plan pursu'd,
And slaughter'd ev'ry king his arm subdu'd,
He would not now have been a man of woes,
Spurn'd by his friends, and tortur'd by his foes;
Had he remained, as he at first began,
The foe of princes, but the friend of man,—
Ah! had he nobly spurn'd the guilty crown,
No human force could e'er have put him down!
For 'tis in vain of princes to complain,
While the old plan of monarchy remain;
How ever man refit, and new arrange,
'Tis but the actors, and the scenes that change;
It is in vain that we the actors blame,
While the whole drama still remain the same:—
Napoleon was, what others were of old,
As Philip sage,— as Alexander bold;
All circumscribed power he disdain'd,
He snatch'd a crown, and like a Caesar reign'd;
Through Europe's numerous states he spread alarm,

And twenty nations fell beneath his arm!
Yet, if there be one, who deserve a crown,
'Tis him whom half the world could scarce put down.

T. He is your favourite then, the thing is plain,
You wish to see him reassume his reign.

D. You much mistake, I wish for no such thing,
Let him be free, but let him not be king.
I Who have long observ'd his ruling plan,
Can hate the king, and yet admire the man
Whose overthrow has but increas'd his fame,
This despots own by trembling at his name;
For well they know while life in him remain,
His soul and genius will in Europe reign;
For this the tyrants form'd the cowardly plan,
To keep an army to secure one man;
But e'en his death would not remove their dread,—
His principles shall live when he is dead:
While that vile race who were by blood restor'd,
Shall only live to see themselves abhor'd;
For France shall execrate from sire to son,
And curse the hated name of Louis Bourbon!
Their only hope's in foreign arms alone,
Twas foreign arms that placed them on the throne:
'Twas foreign arms expell'd that nation's choice,
'Twas foreign arms that stifled Gallia's voice.
Shall Gallia be in such vile bondage held,
And bow to those whom she has twice expell'd;
Who a fierce war 'gainst human knowledge wage,
And play the bigots of the fifteenth age?
Shall such a race command the fiery gaul?—
No!— the prophetic muse predicts their fall;
For France, and Europe now can clearly see,
States must be kingless, ere they can be free!

T. Yet name one state that burst the regal chain,
Which did not wish for monarchy again?
Rome slew her Caesar, but it would not do,
She sigh'd for Empire, and for Emperor too!
And England too of a much later date,
Her king beheaded to subdue her fate;
But mark!— no sooner was the father gone,
Than she with bursts of joy receiv'd his son!
Nor did proud France do either less, or more,
Than kill a King to have an Emperor!—

D. I own there's too much truth in what you say,
But states grow wise by what have pass'd away;
Whate'er was practis'd in a former school,
Thank heaven, there's one exception to that rule;
Columbia, wisely scorns imperial state,
And daily grows more wise,—more rich,—more great.

Then, if one state can do without a king,
'Tis plain enough, a King's a useless thing.
No royal tyrant there, man's rights assail,
There no base aristocracy prevail;
For no such orders fair Columbia rules,
She owns no pension'd knaves, or titled fools;
Her laws accord with nature's glorious plan,
By which her sons enjoy the rights of man.
There all unite in one great family,
Resolving to be happy, and be free;
Proud of those laws, their liberties sustain,
Seal'd with the blood of tens of thousands slain;
Yet, cheaply purchas'd with such sacrifice,
Since universal freedom is the prize!

T. What star is this that rises to my sight,—
Swells fast in magnitude, and grows more bright;
Through every state extending light, and heat,
And seems to bode some change in Europe's fate?—

D. 'Tis reason's light,—an intellectual sun,
Whose influence, none but fools and tyrant's shun:—
'Tis human knowledge, and a sense of right,
That burst upon us like a flood of light;
And if the people only persevere,
All love to princes soon will disappear.
And every tyrant shall be made to feel,
That intellect can not be crush'd by steel!
Never shall justice re-assume her reign;
And men shall sigh for happiness in vain:
But day by day his miseries shall increase,
And states shall bleed in war, or weep in peace;
Laws shall be cobwebs, when opposed to pow'r,
But steel when used to oppress the poor;
Until the Kingdoms change their present plan,
For systems founded on the Rights of Man;
Till every man complete shall have a voice,
To exercise his freedom in his choice
Of who shall rule: and who shall legislate,
Those vital laws on which depends his fate.
This would the miseries of the world assuage,
And bring about the promised golden age.
For then, and NOT TILL THEN, shall JUSTICE REIGN
With PEACE and PLENTY smiling in her train.

FINIS

Queen of the Isles (1820)
Tune: Erin gobragh

O haste, Caroline, haste, o'er the wide water,
And bless all thy people, once more with thy smile,
That people who wept o'er the Tomb of thy Daughter;
Await the return of the Queen of the Isles.
Ah? why dost thou wander in grief and dejection,
And why art thou number'd among the exiles,
While Britons remain with unchanged affection,
For Brunswick's fair Daughter the Queen of the Isles?

When thy ship to our shore, by a breeze shall be driven,
Our love shall protect thee from treachery's toils,
For Britons have sworn that no power under heaven,
Shall tear from their hearts the lov'd Queen of the Isles.
Thy foes have long threaten'd thy Union to sever,
And to blast they fair fame with their falsehood and wit,
But shall guilt over innocence triumph? No, never,
Our hearts are the Throne of the Queen of the Isles.

Our love is now fix'd upon thee, and no other,
The foul tongue of Slander, no longer beguiles;
We, who lov'd the daughter, will cherish the Mother,
The lawful, Legitimate Queen of the Isles.
Then Caroline, haste to thy high destination.
Thy purity o'er thy detracters prevails,
Accept from thy people the kind invitation;
Who long to proclaim thee, the Queen of the Isles.

'London', from *The Muse's Wreath* (1827)

London! when will thy encroachments end?
Must every valley rise, and mountain bend?
Must fields and gardens yield on every side,
And shall no boundaries restrain thy pride?
Ah! whither would'st thou stretch thy lengthing arms?
Thy usurpations fill me with alarms.
Dost thou believe that time cannot destroy
And crumble thee to dust? so once thought TROY!.
And so thought BABYLON of mighty fame,
Of which no wreck remain except the name!
And CARTHAGE too, once great in arms like thee,
And like thee too, the mistress of the sea,
Has disappear'd, and left no trace behind
To satisfy the antiquarian's mind;
And future ages shall for thee inquire,
As we now for Carthage, Thebes, and Tigre!
The learned then, when ask'd where LONDON stood,
Shall answer, 'where yon cattle crop their food!'
   But 'tis not my intention to presage
The revolutions of a future age;
Let other wights, who love to prophesy
The woes that may befal posterity,
Foretel the changes that are yet to come,
As ancient bards foretold the fate of Rome!
The present ills are quite enough for me,
Without anticipating fate's decree.
While liberty and labours *due* are mine,
At fate's decrees my soul shall ne'er repine.
O, liberty! thou bright celestial maid!
To thee all ages have their homage paid;
For thee the patriot has rais'd his voice,
Amidst eternal snows and rocks of ice!
The present is a speculating age;
Go on, then, builders! and exhaust your rage:
In building let your capital be spent;
Let LONDON daily grow in her extent;
Build up the space; let Bath and London join!
Extend her to Newcastle on the Tyne!
Let all our cities be together thrown,
And make old England one imperial town;
Then, like the bold Chinese, build on the flood,
But spare, oh! spare, one spot! spare HORNSEY WOOD!
   Great Terminus*! 'tis thee whom I invoke,

* The god who presides over boundaries.

O shield me from that pestitential smoke,
That over London in dark clouds arise,
To suffocate the lungs and blind the eyes;
Which in the summer darkens half the light,
And turns a winter's day to darkest night!
Grant this request, – O, grant the muse's prayer!
And let her breathe in peace the wholesome air.

From, 'The Co-operator's Catechism,' *Associate and Co-operative Mirror* (1830) (A dialogue between Jack Tellall, a Co-operator, and Tom Seekout)

1. *The Co-operative Society*

Seekout	What do you mean by Co-operation?
Tellall	The assisting each other to obtain or produce any object.
Seekout	Ah, but I want to know what the Co-operation is, we hear so much about. In fact it is in every man's mouth – in every newspaper and magazine.
Tellall	Oh, I understand you – you want to know something about the Co-operation that is occupying the attention of my brother workmen, who have formed a Co-operative society in our own village.
Seekout	Yes! do tell me what it means; for, hang me, if I do not find out some new way of living, I stand a fair chance of going to the poor-house, with my wife and family, like poor Bill Nowork.
Tellall	Co-operation, such as I perceive it to be, is a new road to obtain plenty of work, plenty of food, and as many good clothes as any body can wear.
Seekout	You don't say so, Jack – my coat's out at elbows, and button my jacket, if my belly isn't pinched in like the squire's greyhound. As to work, I can get plenty o'that, but then there's not as many ha'pence as will buy a bellyfull for Betty and our two brats – poor things!
Tellall	Tom, I know you are a shrewd fellow, and can see your own interest as well as any body, so come along with me, and we will talk this matter over a cup of tea, along with my wife, who expects me home before I go to the society. You know I am a member, and it is my duty to look after our affairs, or I shall be left behind in a knowledge of what is going on.
Seekout	Pooh! let your wife take her tea, and we'll go to Timothy Longscores, at the sign of the pipe and puncheon, and drink success to Co-operation, the short road to plenty.
Tellall	No, Tom; I have learnt a better way of spending my time, than making a beast of myself and starving my wife and children.

Seekout Aye, Jack, I forgot that you don't enjoy yourself with your friends as you used to do.

Tellall There, Tom, you are quite out, for I enjoy myself along with my friends more than ever I did; and never quarrel about who's to pay the reckoning with Timothy Longscores; and if you did the same, you would be a happier man than you are now, with a starving wife and children, and no fire-side to warm them.

Seekout Well, well; it wasn't always so. Come – I'll go with you home, and we'll wish success to Co-operation all the same.

Tellall You don't seem so happy, Tom, as when you had plenty of work and good wages.

Seekout No; the times are altered.

Tellall No, they're not; only you begin to feel the effects of having worked for another, without enjoying the full fruit of your own labour. No – the times are not altered – but it's time they were and the time will come when they will be, or else Co-operation is not founded in truth.

Seekout You cheer us, Tom, with this word Co-operation, now tell me what it is.

Tellall Yes – Cooperation is every one labouring – every one exchanging labour for labour – every one having plenty of food, clothes, and good lodging. In short, it is enjoying every thing, and contributing to every thing, equally; so that there shall be no distinction between the rich and the poor; the idle and the industrious; the ignorant and the learned. Neither will man nor woman be unequal in their rights, as members of society.

Seekout That is a beautiful dream, Jack – if you could show us how such things may be brought about, why, I would not mind saying good bye to Tim Longscores, and all the beer at the pipe and puncheon. For I begin to think it cannot be right, that I and poor Bob Neverdone, should work all day picking turnips for sixpence a day, and be obliged to spend it afterwards at our master's tommy-shop in Syston. You know, Jack, I am a framework-knitter, and can make as good stockings as any man.

Tellall Tom, it's no dream, but clear indisputable reality. Don't you see that lot of fine folks yonder, coming home, dressed better than ever we were at our wedding days; they are going to sit down to a good dinner, and wine, after it.

Seekout Ah, that I do, and see master and his young ladies among them.

Tellall Well, Tom, how did they get those fine clothes? Why, there's Miss, with a pair of lace ancle stockings, the very same you made three months back.

Seekout — Sure enough, I made them for her father, old Getall, who paid me the lowest wages of any that I have taken since I worked at the frame.

Tellall — Well, but did you make a pair for your wife when you made them; you know the cotton cost a trifle?

Seekout — Me? no – I worked hard to get my wages to buy my victuals; and when I got them, I had not time to eat them quietly, I was so pushed to get my work done by the week's end.

Tellall — Don't you think, Tom, if you had time to make a pair of lace ancle stockings for your wife, that she would wear them if you made them.

Seekout — To be sure she would, and has as good a leg and foot to show them off with, as Miss there. What better is Miss's foot than my darling Bessy's? It is but flesh and blood, it grows old and perhaps uglier, and will rot at last too.

Tellall — I can't tell you; but if you ask the parson, he will tell you to conduct yourself lowly and reverently to your betters.

Seekout — Betters! – If you mean those that never put their hands to any kind of work, why Jem Donothing, that went to the poor-house last week must be on a footing with Squire Cullpenny and Parson Tenthpig, for there is ne'er a one of them that does ought but talk about what does not belong to them.

Tellall — I think, for my part that our betters, if there be any, are those that do more good to our neighbours than we do – that assist the unfortunate and distressed as much as their means will allow – that don't talk about the vices of others without correcting their own – that seek to enable people to live honestly, and prevent that distress which obliges unfortunate people to commit crimes – that respect the honest man when he is clad in rags, and do unto others what they would others should do unto them.

Seekout — Well – we agree on that score.

Tellall — If you could work for yourself and family, independent of old Getall, would you?

Seekout — Yes – what do you ask that for? You know I cannot spare money to pay for a pound of cotton yarn, therefore how can I work, independent of those persons who pay me my wages at the week's end.

Tellall — Is it any matter to you, whether you work for one man, or the whole village so as you are paid for your labour?

Seekout — No, to be sure; when I work, all I want is to receive money for my work when it is done; I don't care whether my time is occupied in working for fifty people or one, so as I am kept constantly employed.

Tellall	Then suppose our Co-operative society, there are forty members in it, were to elect you a member, and give you work, which they would sell or dispose of, would you work as well for them as your present master?
Seekout	That I would; but tell me, if they sell the stockings I made, what would become of the money?
Tellall	It would go into the common stock to purchase more cotton, and pay more wages.
Seekout	But, tell me, how did your society get money to purchase the cotton, first, and to pay my wages: you know that it takes a great deal of money to do that.
Tellall	Why, when we formed our Co-operative society, we agreed to pay five pounds per member, by weekly instalments or subscriptions of not less than sixpence. Some of us paid more than sixpence a week, so that we were sooner done paying than others. You know there are forty-four members, so we raised two hundred and thirty pounds very soon, for we had no drawbacks. With this money we set some of our members to work, and we sold their work to the public with a small profit, yet more than covered our expenses. We can always afford a smaller profit than other dealers, because we have not fine houses, horses, coaches, servants, and such like to pay for. And I hope to see the day when we shall have money enough to buy the best machinery in the country, and land too, and then we can live on it, and laugh at those who now laugh at us.
Seekout	Aye but how can I afford to pay sixpence a week.
Tellall	Reckon! How many pints of beer do you drink between Saturday night and Saturday night?
Seekout	One a day, sometimes on Saturday or Sunday morning two or three.
Tellall	Well, we will say six pints of beer a week, that is, at two-pence a pint, one shilling a week in beer. Now just stop a few weeks from your beer, and you'll pay the money fast enough I warrant you.
Seekout	Oh, but if you stop my beer I cannot do my work; it strengthens me, and then it is good for the body.
Tellall	Strengthens you! stuff – it makes a beast of you every Saturday night, and then you're in bed all Sunday. No man; a good belly full of crowdy or beef would strengthen you far more than beer.
Seekout	Poh! I don't believe that, what I feel like a man when I have my pint of beer.
Tellall	Yes, and like a child too when you can't get another. You saw

Tom Lightfoot when he was training for 100 mile walking-match, now he never touched any thing but his victuals and spring water. And Thumping Ned, when he was training to fight Alexander Scott, who died the day after the fight; he never touched any drink but water; and surely his strength was greater than yours. It is a pity, such fine strong fellows should disgrace themselves, with such a savage kind of work as murder. Tom, do you think you'll ever be as strong as these chaps, with drinking beer and such like?

Seekout It is very true, Jack. There is some reason in what you say. Hang me if I don't put my two-pence bye, and try water to my dinner to-morrow.

Tellall If you do that for a few weeks, you'll say I am the best friend you ever had. For you'll soon find out, that beer does no good to any body but the brewer, and Squire Cullpenny who grows the barley.

Seekout Well, we'll see what's to be done. But tell me who takes the money and the goods which you say are common stock. I don't rightly understand what you mean by common stock.

Tellall The property of the society belongs to all the members in common, that is equally. This property is called common stock, whether it be money goods or lands. There are officers appointed by the members of the society, to look after and take care of the things, and manage all the affairs of the society. When we formed the society, the first thing we did was to appoint a Secretary, to write down in a book all the things we agreed to do, every time we met. This book we call a minute book. It contains a report of all the proceedings and the names of the members as they were elected. Some other time you shall see this book. After appointing a Secretary we appointed a Treasurer to take care of the money; you know him well.

Seekout Indeed, what's his name?

Tellall George Careful, a steady sober fellow, and although he never was much of a favourite with Parson Tenthpig, and the dissenting preacher Moses Smoothface, because he thought they preached for the loaves and fishes, and not for their flocks; still our treasurer has always been an honest, frank and upright, fellow, and we take care to keep him from temptation by always having security for our money, and making him produce the cash in hand every meeting night.

Seekout Then what does the treasurer do with the money?

Tellall He brings it with him every meeting night, and the committee order him in writing, to pay it to the secretary, as it is wanted to pay for cotton and other things, or to pay the wages of those that are employed. This way, the Secretary knows and keeps an account of the sums that are paid away, and as he gathers the money and pays it to the Treasurer, who takes care of it, and pays it only on an order, we are always acquainted with the amount of our receipts and expenses. We save a great deal of trouble this way, and keep satisfactory accounts of all property.

Seekout You said a committee order the treasurer to make payments – what do you mean by a committee?

Tellall A committee is a body of officers appointed to perform a particular duty. And as there are several different duties to be performed, there are several different committees. We have appointed three persons as a committee for managing the accounts of the society; also three persons as a committee to superintend the management of the stocking manufactures. This committee purchase the cotton when they think it is wanted. They set hands to work or discharge others from work. They order the secretary to pay certain bills, and the wages of the workmen. They make monthly reports to the society of what they have done. They keep an account of their transactions in writing, and a stock account of the property which they manage. They fix the prices, the articles are to be sold at; in fact, they act every way as managers of the particular department they are appointed to. There is also a committee for barter or exchanging goods with societies, or between the members. This committee knows what the trade of every member is, and whether he be employed by the society, or want employment, or wish to exchange his labour for some other member's labour. This committee also keeps an account of all the trading, or commercial transactions of the society. They take all the goods, as soon as they are manufactured, under their care, and keep accounts of all the sales of the manufactures, and like all other committees, make a report to the society every month or oftener, of their transactions. There is also a committee for education and improvement. This is a very useful committee.

Seekout Excellent! Jack, I will come to your meeting to-night if you please.

Tellall Very well, we'll go together.

II *The Co-operative Community*

Tellall — Your character a few weeks ago, was that of being a drunken, and extravagant, but an affectionate father. Then, from your opinions held by you at that time, in consequence of the circumstances that created those opinions, you were compelled to be all that you were represented to be. And would have been till now, perhaps even worse, if we had not had our dialogue or conversation together, about the uselessness of drinking liquor to make you strong; and paying a few visits to our Co-operative Society, where you saw a number of men and women, framework knitters like yourself, happy, and enjoying each others conversation, which you recollect was interesting, and carried on without displaying any angry feelings about the faults and errors of others.

Seekout — Then, if I cannot avoid possessing the character that I have, and doing the acts that I do, nor having the opinions I have, you cannot blame me for what I was. In fact, if I was to murder somebody this instant, you could not blame me for doing so; because I was compelled from the motives created in me to commit murder. In short, I am fated to be what I am, or may be, therefore it is needless for me to make any efforts to be otherwise than what chance may make me.

Tellall — Although you are not to blame for being what you are, if that be hurtful; or deserving of praise for what you are, if that be good; still you are not to suppose that because of these facts, no steps are to be taken to prevent you from committing murder, or doing other hurtful things. There cannot be a question that you are fated to do that which circumstances compel you to do; and this is a most fortunate thing for yourself and society. For as circumstances compel you to do good or evil, we must select such circumstances as compel you to do good only, and remove those that compel you to do harm, so that you shall not be surrounded with one single circumstance, which shall create in you a motive for doing harm, and surround you with circumstances only, which shall compel you to do nothing but good, from the hour of your birth to the day of your death.

Seekout — Indeed. How will you contrive that?

Tellall — By placing you in a Co-operative Community.

Seekout — Eh, what, a Co-operative Community?

Tellall — Yes. A Co-operative Community.

Seekout — And pray what is a Co-operative community? which, you say, is to prevent me from doing hurtful things, and will compel me to do nothing but good things.

Tellall A Co-operative community is a society of persons living together, in a large palace, or squares, on terms of the most perfect equality, as one family, loving each other as brothers and sisters. Each person contributes a share in the labour that is required to produce all the comforts and luxuries they enjoy; every one of the members in a community have two nice, clean, healthy, and convenient rooms, one to sleep in, and one to set in; all the children of the members are educated together in a large nursery, where they are brought up in perfect ignorance of crime, the little darlings smile and play with each other, as naturally as young lambs.

. . . .

Tellall Listen – In the Co-operative Community you have a large public hall for dining in, finer too than the town hall, where you will go to dine in the company of friends whom you esteem – then as you have contributed your portion of labour to the common storehouse of the community, you will be entitled to have in exchange your dinner, breakfast, or other meals, cooked by the labour of another person, who gets in exchange for it some of your stockings, or other things in the storehouse. You know, "a fair exchange is no robbery."

Seekout That is like me and my wife together now. She cooks the dinner, makes the clothes, and cleans the house, and I work for the victuals, clothes, and furniture. Upon my word, I see that we all might live in a large family with industry, and civility, as easily as we do in small ones, and have plenty of good company too to make us happy.

Tellall Yes, and company of a very different stamp to what we enjoy amongst our acquaintances now. We should be all well educated then – every one having a hundred times as much knowledge of the principles of society, and human nature, as the best of us now possess. We should be above the fear of want, and enjoy more real comforts, and luxuries, than the richest Lord in the land.

Seekout Now Jack you're dreaming again – I cannot yet see how all these things can take place amongst a set of poor workmen, who are looked on as the scum of the earth. Although I see we can have some things that we have not at present, still, when you talk of the comforts, and luxuries enjoyed by the Lords of the soil, I begin to think you're not in earnest.

Tellall I am not surprised at that, for it is so far above our present condition, you think we can never be better off than hired mechanics all our lives. The only difference between men's minds is their education; therefore when we are all educated alike there cannot be great shades of difference between our minds, and as to the difference of condition, that will be done away with too, if there be an equality of condition established throughout society, which must take place eventually, in spite of all that may be said to the contrary.

Seekout What do you mean by equality of condition; are we all to be as rich as lords, or are all to be as poor as we are now?

Tellall We shall not be as rich as lords, and yet we shall enjoy and consume far more useful things than they do now. A lord has the sole possession of his property; now this he has no right to have, when other persons are starving about him, for you must recollect that it is unnecessary for the happiness of the working classes, that any set of men should retain exclusive possession of those things that they do not produce themselves. Indeed it is a violation of the laws of nature, to take possession to the exclusion of others, of the land we walk on. As well might the parliament-men pass an act, giving themselves possession of the air we breathe, the light from the sun, or the waters from the clouds.

Seekout Well, but if the few folks that make laws for the government of the people, could take possession of those things they would very soon pass acts of parliament, giving them that possession. It is from no sense of justice that they do not do so.

Tellall Very true Tom; they have made laws to prevent every body but themselves, or those they choose, from fishing in the rivers and lakes; and laws to prevent every body but themselves from killing hares, and partridges in the fields; and to prevent every body but themselves from pulling a few nuts in the woods; and laws to prevent every body but themselves from sitting down on the grass, or walking across a field; even the light in the houses, and the cubic feet of air they contain are indirectly theirs and taxed. In fact we cannot say we have a right to stand on the earth for every inch of it belongs to some one or other.

Seekout All this is very true – we cannot dispute it. But we are quitting the subject of equality of condition.

Tellall It appears necessary that all persons both men, and women, under a highly cultivated state of society, should have equal means of enjoyment, which necessarily requires that each person should contribute as much as they can to the amount of wealth, or common property, possessed by the people. Each person should be entitled to wear the best clothes that can be made; each person should be entitled to inhabit the best apartments or dwelling that may be constructed; each person should be entitled to eat the best food that may be prepared; each person should be entitled to have, and be given, the best mental, and physical education that may be known; each child should be the child of the whole nation, and every man and woman should be as a father and a mother to it, and every one should be as a brother or sister to one and other.

Seekout Ah Jack! What a time it will be before the people can go through the necessary changes in their opinions and habits, before they can bring these things about.

Tellall Yes, it is true the steps between that state of society, and the present, are many, and far between, and must be very progressive, for, before we can effect those changes that are necessary, we must change the circumstances that surround us, which form a part of the present society of the world, or we need not expect the beautiful results that we anticipate.

Seekout Yes, but I think we shall even then have many things to be dissatisfied about; as for instance, you cannot give every one at dinner the best of every thing on table, or can you clothe them all equally well.

Tellall These things are deserving of our consideration, and like other evils, attending old society, may be readily prevented in a community of property, labour, and condition. It is quite unnecessary for us to make or cultivate any but the best of everything that can be made. For there cannot be any inducement to make bad articles, if there be not any body who will be indolent enough to be contented with them. And as to food, we have only to make a superabundance of those kinds we most esteem, and the desire to possess exclusively any particular part will form no impediment to the gratification of all of us; besides the mind will be so trained as to prevent those degrading tastes existing in it, which at present form a constant source of misery to the possessor of them. If we are trained to seek the means of gratifying others as a source of pleasure, in preference to seeking the gratification of our own tastes, we shall prefer giving to others those objects which they desire or want for their gratification, in preference to preserving them for ourselves.

Seekout Yes, I can readily understand, that the best of every thing may be produced, in preference to manufacturing or preparing, as we do now, many articles of different qualities to suit the unequal means of various persons to purchase them. I see clearly, that the inequality of condition now prevailing through society, causes the sale of the variety of good and bad articles, that are made for the public markets. And also that our training, or education will create in us the desire to afford pleasure to others, as a source of happiness for ourselves.

Tellall Then fancy a party of workmen, and workwomen, for in a perfect state of Co-operation, we shall all, when young, be workmen and workwomen, sitting down to a table covered with an abundance of the best and wholesomest food that can be procured, without the fear of wanting the things most necessary to promote our happiness, and waited on by the younger portion of the people in our community, who will have dined previously to us, and on whom we shall have attended, in the true spirit, of an exchange of labour. Can you fancy that the workpeople shall be discontented, and seeking to get possession to the exclusion of others, of one bit of meat in preference to another! Look Tom on this picture – (shewing a picture) see the smoaking joints of meat and vegetables – the clean table cloth – the well dressed people beaming with content, and the gay, happy youths around, reflecting in their smiles, the pleasure felt by the whole party – see how anxious they are to be of use, and assist every one seated before them – such happy people all human beings may become.

Seekout But whose children are those young people waiting on the older guests – are they sons and daughters of a few of them, or are they children of other persons?

Tellall They may or may not be the particular children of those at table, it matters not, for all the children belong to the community, and know not who are their fathers and mothers, and yet know that all the adults or grown people are as fathers and mothers to them, and they are as sisters and brothers to each other, loving without distinction of kindred, therefore without the chance of family distinctions, which are prejudicial to the happiness of the people.

Seekout What, not know your own father and mother, nor your brothers and sisters; why, you will have no parental or fillial affection.

Tellall It is not necessary that there should be any, for it springs out of many associated feelings which are acquired by parents and children, because they are told, that they are the parents or children of particular persons. You had no knowledge of your birth, that the father and mother you had were really such, or that your brothers and sisters were really from the same womb as yourself. You are taught to love these relations, in preference to other people, because they are your kindred, and you weep and experience aggravated pain when any thing befalls them; you show a preference to them, and are trained to love your neighbours less than your relations, yet your neighbours possess all the valuable qualities of human nature, and as members of the human family or society in which you live, are quite as useful to the community. The ties of kindred frequently prevent you from doing your duty to your fellow beings, they sear up the heart against that universal benevolence which should form the prominent part of your disposition, and render you much oftener uncomfortable than happy.

Seekout But then the mother at least has a natural attachment to her child. Surely that is not the result of associated feelings.

Tellall Yes, but we have yet to ascertain, how far this pleasing feeling experienced by the mother is useful to the child in after life, and to society. And whether it does not arise from physical circumstances, independent of any moral feeling. There is no question that our attachment and aversion to objects depend on the amount of pleasing, and painful feelings experienced by us, and excited by the objects, whether a child or a neighbour; therefore we must look for the cause of this affection in these circumstances, and ascertain whether it is useful to encourage this maternal feeling of attachment beyond the period of suckling. You know we are to do that which is best for the happiness of individuals – therefore think about what we have just discussed. It involves many considerations of great importance to society, and may hereafter occupy it when considering the utility of permanent marriages between the sexes.

The Working Classes come to their Senses*

London, September 16, 1833

The following letter is humbly addressed by the governed, to their governors, the noble lords and honourable and right honourable gentlemen of both Houses of Parliament, and delivered by one of that numerous body.

My Lords and Gentlemen,

'We gratefully acknowledge and sincerely thank you for the care and solicitude with which you watched over us, while we were in that wretched state of insanity which rendered us at once so helpless and so miserable, and for the extraordinary pains you took, sparing neither trouble nor time, to restore us to our proper senses. We, also, now we have recovered the right use of our senses, admire the ingenuity you displayed in furnishing the various means by which you so happily brought about that glorious consummation.

We certainly did think, at times, my Lords and Gentlemen, while we were withering under the torture of the lash! or clanking our chains in our solitary dungeons! or being knocked on the head by your bludgeons! trampled under foot by your horses! cut down by your sabres! hung up by the neck like dogs! or fired upon with musketry and cannon! that you were too severe, and that the remedies were too powerful, desperate as our disorder was. But we now see, and are free to confess, that you were the best judges of our case; and that your long practice and great experience enabled you to decide that nothing short of the means you so judiciously employed, could restore us to the proper use of our mutual faculties; which alone could enable us "to take our affairs into our own hands." This, my Lords and Gentlemen, you have done, and we now release you from your painful and arduous task; and as a token of our gratitude and esteem, we allow you free admission into any of our unions, trading associations, equitable labour exchanges, &c. where you will be carefully instructed in some useful trade or calling, which will enable you to meet without dismay that wide and sweeping revolution which is fast approaching, and which will

*Poor Man's Guardian, 21 September 1833

exterminate every class of idlers as certainly as the bees destroy the drones!

But if, my Lords and Gentlemen, you decline to accept this offer, which is the very best we have in our power to make, you are perfectly free to go to whatever part of the world you please; and be assured that wherever you may be destined to roam, or however wide the ocean that shall part us, neither time, change of circumstances, nor distance, will cause the working classes of England to forget their old masters'.

I am, my Lords and Gentlemen,
In the sight of God, and in the scale of your fellow man, your equal
ALLEN DAVENPORT

Property in Danger*

To the Editor of the Times

SIR – "The Church in danger", used to be the cry of the Conservatives, whenever any liberal measure was proposed for the benefit of any portion of the people who may have been groaning under unjust and exclusive laws; and as long as "Church and King mobs" could be called to their assistance, no reform could be brought about that would equalize the laws and ameliorate the condition of the people at large. But since that cry has lost its charm, and no individual pays the least attention to it except the Conservatives themselves, a new cry, "Property in danger!" is raised; and all those who tried to obtain such reforms as would enable the labourer to enjoy a greater portion of the fruits of his labour, are called "Destructives". I am quite sure that this new cry will have no more effect on the working classes than the old one; but, as it may inspire some of the middle classes with fear, it is a sufficient reason, perhaps, that some notice should be taken of it; and in doing this, Sir, it will be necessary to make a few remarks on your conduct in setting up this new cry. For in setting up this new cry, you prove, notwithstanding all your great and shining abilities, and the facility which you possess in acquiring every description of knowledge, that you are either ignorant or wilfully inconsistent on this particular subject. In the first place, then, you profess to be a Reformer, and say, "May we perish, if ever we abandon the principles we profess."

Now, let us take a short view of this property question, beginning with the passing of the Reform Bill, or *New Magna Charta*, as it was called, and for which you was the leading champion. Pray Sir, was there no attack on property in passing that bill? Was the breaking up of sixty boroughs, no revulsion of property? Do you not know sir, that the property invested in those boroughs by the borough-mongers, previous to the passing of the Reform Bill, was as sacred in the eye of the law as their landed estates? If you do not know this, then you are ignorant only; but if you do know this, and know also that no reform, however trivial, can be brought about without a sacrifice of property to somebody, you are worse than ignorant, for you are wilfully inconsistent; and that is the worst thing a public writer can be guilty of. How far property was in danger by the passing of the

*Poor Man's Guardian, 17 January 1835

Reform Bill, one instance will be sufficient to show. Lord Monson, I believe that was the name, a short time previous to the passing of the Reform Bill, purchased a borough for 180,000*l.*; but after the Reform Bill had passed, he was reported to have offered the same property for 100,000*l.*; here, then, was a clear loss to Lord Monson of 80,000*l.* by the Reform Bill. Do you call this nothing? And who can deny that the abolition of the tithe system would be an attack on property? Individuals in this case would lose from 500*l.* to 5,000*l.* annually. The same may be said with respect to corporations, they cannot be reformed without loss of property. Again, you could not abolish the sinecure and pension list, for which, to your credit, you are a very warm advocate, without attacking property. In a word, every Act of Parliament that passes puts somebody's property in danger.

Perhaps you will say that all these institutions are so corrupted and abused that they become nuisances, and the spirit of the age demands their abolition. To which I agree. But why, then, set up the cry of "Property in danger?" But what institutions, among all others, require reform more than those that regulate landed property? Is it not in the power of the landowners, protected as they are by the laws of a primogeniture and Corn Laws, to withhold the means of life from the people, almost as completely as a besieging army may destroy a garrison by starvation, by cutting off all supply? Why should such institutions be held inviolable? The abolition of the laws of primogeniture and the Corn Laws would be no more an attack on property than any of the other reforms which I have enumerated. Is it right that 70,000 persons should hold all the land, together with all the mines, coal pits, fisheries, &c., in the country, to the exclusion of twenty-five millions of individuals. If this be right, all that I have to say is, that all other reforms are wrong. But, of all the attacks on property since the days of the Protestant Reformation, that recently made on the property of the poor by passing the Poor Law Amendment Bill was the most unjust, the most cruel, and the most base. It was bad enough to rob the poor of their property in the moor lands and common fields, but to deprive them of the means without which they could not exist amounts to murder. And if the Duke of Wellington is not dead to every principle of justice, and every feeling of humanity, as well as blind to every thing in the spirit of sound policy, he will immediately declare himself willing to repeal that wicked, cruel, and savage law.

To your very great credit, Sir, on this measure, at any rate, you was constantly on the side of the poor and I am happy to see that, however you have changed in other respects, you continue a staunch and powerful opponent to that terrible and murderous act of tyranny and oppression.

And now, Sir, I think I have said enough to convince you that there can be no reform of any description without involving in it the question of property; and, being convinced of that, you will see the propriety of dropping the cry of "Property in danger."

It is true Mr Owen professes to be able, if permitted, to revolutionize the whole world without injuring the property of a single individual. But Mr Owen belongs to another world – the "New Moral World." We cannot dispute what he can do in another world, but we know such things cannot be done in our old world without injury to somebody.

Your most obedient and humble servant.

5, Moor-lane, City, ALLEN DAVENPORT

Dec. 16, 1834.

Simultaneous Meetings*

"Nil actum reputans; si quid supereset agendum."
To the Editor of the Poor Man's Guardian

SIR – It has long been a matter of surprise to me, that the people (particularly the working people) have never adopted the plan of simultaneous meetings. Had the Consolidated Trades' Unions acted upon such a system, when their six brothers of Dorchester were (as it is now proved) illegally convicted, and unjustly sentenced to seven years' transportation beyond the seas, how different would have been the result. When the Unions of London, on the 19th April, 1833, so promptly met in Copenhagen-fields, and boldly, yet with the most perfect order, marched in tens of thousands through the streets of the metropolis, to the Secretary of State's office, to deliver their petition with their own hands, every branch of that tremendous Union, in every part of the country, should have met on the same day, and for the same purpose, and have rested upon their arms (to use a military phrase) till the unjust and cruel sentence had been annulled. Had the Unions acted thus, I feel confident that the six victims of illegal power would never have been forced from the bosoms of their families, and their native land!

Let us, then, profit by experience – let us hasten to employ those means to recal them, which, had they been sooner adopted, would have prevented their banishment! Simultaneous meetings would also prevent the Government from surrounding and overawing the people, during their deliberations at great public meetings, with the military, which prevents thousands of patriotic, but timid, persons, from attending such necessary assemblies. How should it be otherwise, when we have seen in London, on the bare notice of an open-air meeting, the metropolis surrounded by at least 20,000 soldiers, with the necessary number of cannon; and, perhaps, not less than 10,000 policemen, special constables, and other persons, all armed with cutlasses and firearms, with some placeman, pensioner, or clergyman of the Church of England at their head, ready at any given moment to cry "havoc!" and let slip the dogs of war among the peaceful and legally assembled multitude!

Now this great military power could not be brought to bear against the people, if they were on every great occasion to meet simultaneously; for, if

*Poor Man's Guardian, 18 July 1835

it be necessary to call 30,000 armed men to surround and overawe the people of the metropolis, Manchester, Birmingham, and most of the great towns and cities in the country, would be left almost free from such military threatenings! so, that wherever the sword of power should be made to usurp the empire of the laws at one point, the people would be enabled to revenge it at another point. For it is a maxim, that never ought to be forgotten, that where power has been exercised above the laws on one single individual, the whole community ought to rise up as one man to revenge the individual cause of their fellow-citizen! And, as to military power, what would all the military and police power of the whole empire be in the hands of the working classes alone, if they were as thoroughly united in heart and hand as their wealthy oppressors!

If the Government think it necessary, on every trivial occasion, to martial all its forces, and summon all its powers, in the defence of the property of the rich, why should not the sons and daughters of labour exert all their ingenuity, and call all their energies into action, to defend the fruits of their toil, and that heaven-born liberty, without which life is but misery and pain. The rich man has no more right to invade the liberty of the poor man, than the poor man has to invade the rich man's property!

I feel assured, that if such a *moral rising of the people*, which I here contemplate, were to take place throughout England, Scotland, and Ireland, and a demand made for the unconditional recal of the six Dorchester Labourers! the six Unionists!? the six Englishmen!!! – with a firm nerve and a loud voice – the Government would not, could not, resist the demand. And when they shall return to their native shore, what better plan could be devised to welcome their return, and to celebrate the happy event, than by honouring them with a simultaneous but a peaceful *rising up* throughout the land.

5 Moor-lane, London ALLEN DAVENPORT

July 13, 1835

'Universal Suffrage'*

The time has now fully arrived, that the question of Universal Suffrage ought to be made the test of honest and honourable feeling to every individual who shall, at the approaching general election, set up pretensions to, and claim the right of, becoming a representative of the people in the great legislative council of the nation. What a moral phenomenon – what an anomaly, in a civilized state like that of England, would be exhibited, should any candidate so far forget the principles of justice, the injunctions of religion, and the claims of humanity, as to dare look the millions of honest and industrious artisans and labourers in the face, of whom he may be surrounded, and tell them that he cannot consciencously pledge himself to vote, in his legislative capacity, in favour of that popular question!

What would such a declaration amount to? Would it not be tantamount to saying that four-fifths of the adult population of this country are either idiots, lunatics, or criminals in the eye of the law? Who will deny that it would? After such a declaration, the following questions may be very appropriately put to such a candidate, by those who have no vote in the election:–

Sir, – I have no vote – no share in making the laws and neither do any one ask me to give my assent to any law that is enacted by the Legislature, though it should effect my property, my liberty, and my life! Am I, under such circumstances, responsible to such laws? And ought I to be punished for their infraction? Should the candidate reply in the affirmative, you will see at once that he is prepared to sacrifice political justice, civil right, and social comfort, to narrow-minded selfishness, speculative views, and family aggrandizement, and is determined to *stick to his order*! He is not the man to represent the millions – he is not the man which the spirit of the age requires.

I am not going to say, that if an unrepresented individual commits an outrage on society, or injures one of its members, that he should not be punished. But I do contend that it would look more like justice, if society were to execute popular judgement, and inflict summary punishment on the offender, than that he should be punished by a law enacted by those in the choice of whom he had neither directly nor indirectly vote or interest in

**The London Democrat*, 8 June 1839.

the whole matter. No better definition than this can be given to the word *slave*!

Not but the person who should be so punished, may have to undergo a more severe sentence, than would have been inflicted on him by law, but that is not the question: it is for justice that I am contending; if we cannot compel our tyrants to be just by mild and moral means, what ought we to do?

'Shall we tamely lick the foot upraised to trample on our rights, shake our chains, and find melody in their horrid clank?' Or shall we meet the enemy of our rights in a trial of strength, and prefer being buried in one common grave beneath the ruins of our country, if they will have so? It is time the working classes should decide on these important questions.

THE

ENGLISH INSTITUTIONS;

AN EDUCATIONAL POEM,

BY ALLEN DAVENPORT,

Author of "Urania," "Life of Spence," &c.

"Hail, glorious science! for thou canst impart,
A charm to humanize the savage heart;
If not for thee this beauteous earth had been
A wilderness : a den of savage men;
Without a language, and without a mind,
With bodies naked, lashed by every wind;
And had not science worked out nature's plan,
The brute had held dominion over man."

LONDON :

PUBLISHED BY JOHN CLEAVE, No. 1, SHOE LANE,
AND MAY BE HAD AT THE BOOKSELLERS.

DEDICATION.

TO JOHN ROBINSON, ESQ.
Founder of the Tower Street Mutual Instruction Society.

SIR,

Who so proper could I select, from among the friends of education, and the advocates of liberal principles, to dedicate an educational poem to, as him who has not only founded a literary and scientific society, but who has also combined all his energies, called every faculty into action, and exerted to the utmost his various and powerful genius, to consolidate and preserve that society, which may with truth be said to be the work of his own hands?

This society, though of very humble pretensions, may now be fairly deemed a branch of that tree of universal knowledge, which is rapidly extending itself over the whole face of Europe and America, and every other part of the world where the light of science has been permitted to penetrate; where inductive philosophy has been allowed to demonstrate facts; and mechanical genius has been suffered to develope its stupendous powers!

What were the wonders of the ancient world, however great, in comparison with those of modern times? and yet, astonishing as are the effects produced by the developments of the human mind, as at present, a future race, by the aid of a scientific mechanical, and moral education, shall as far surpass the present generation, as the present has surpassed every age that has gone before it.

The ubiquity of the printing press—the time-contracting, and space-annihilating railway—the galaxies of burning gas—the life-creating galvanic battery—the Thames tunnel—and the almost miraculous powers of steam—are among the wonders of the present age; but there are yet principles, properties and powers, to be discovered; and a distant posterity having made the discovery, and so highly improved the political, social, and moral condition of man, will look back upon the nineteenth century as a very dull, if not one of the dark ages; and scarcely give credit to the historian who shall hand down to future generations, the history of the institutions, social arrangements, and the principles of the governments, of what are now called civilized nations!

To estimate your value to the cause of general education, it is only necessary to say, that the Tower Street Mutual Instruction Society, has been in existence more than seven years, with a splendid library, and a considerable quantity of apparatus for chemistry, optics, galvanism, &c., with weekly lectures, delivered to the members and friends, and almost daily instructions given to the various classes, on every branch of useful knowledge, for the exceedingly small contribution of *one shilling per quarter!* To which the annals of institutions furnish no example.

This circumstance alone, Sir, would be a splendid monument to your memory, and render the name of JOHN ROBINSON, like that of your late much lamented friend ROLAND DETROSIER, dear to posterity, as your active genius is admired by all who know you and have an opportunity of appreciating your general merits.

But gratitude for favors bestowed, and instruction received, have inspired me with a double motive for thus addressing you; first, to give "honor to whom honor is due;" and secondly to give some small token, that I who have for seven years occupied the presidental chair, have not been entirely inactive. Though I have often blushed for my own insignificance, while observing your indefatigable industry, unceasing perseverance, and steady determinations to overcome what others unfeignedly believed, and loudly proclaimed to be impossibilities! you have been eminently successful in your struggle—your triumph, Sir, is complete—and to have a hundred and thirty disciples highly sensible of your merit, and deeply grateful for the service you have rendered them, is as sweet a reward as your own unsophisticated mind is capable of receiving.

May you live long, attended by prosperity and happiness, and be enabled to continue, as you have hitherto done, your powerful aid in the glorious cause of national education, and civil and religious liberty—is the ardent and sincere wish of,

Sir,
Your obedient and humble Servant,
ALLEN DAVENPORT.

76, Chamber Street, Goodman's Fields, Jan. 1st, 1842.

The English Institutions.

Hail! glorious spirit of eternal light!
Descend and dissipate that mental night,
Whose dreary gloom the human sight defies,
And chains the intellectual energies;
Inspire some master mind with some bright plan,
To cultivate the faculties of man—
Plant in his breast, with a judicious hand,
Such knowledge that his mind can understand.
Let metaphysics moulder on the shelf,
He is the wisest man who knows himself;
Without that knowledge he is but a clod,
Howe'er he may pretend to know his God!
A knowledge of himself will give the clue
To every science that he may pursue;
To analyze the earth, or mete the skies,
And make him virtuous as he grows more wise;
Then he will estimate the power that wrought,
'The fine machinery that creates thought!'
No. shall creation's fairest—sweetest rose,
Remain neglected, and enslaved by those
Whose pride it ought to be to cultivate,
And raise her to the highest moral state;
And make her in the universal school,
Intelligent as she is beautiful;
Then we may yet, in lovely woman find,
As well as angel's form, an angel's mind!
Then shall the rising generation see
The road to happiness—to liberty!
How pleasing to behold the budding rose,
Burst through the calyx and its tints disclose!
To see it blossom and perfume the vale,
And breathe its sweets in every passing gale.
How pleasing to behold the sportive lamb,
To frisk and dance around the bleating dam,
Then fly at tangent and its speed increase,
To join its blithe companions in the chase!
How pleasing to observe, with half-fledged wing,
The little bird cock up his bill to sing,
Then turn his ear to catch the warbling notes,
That come mellifluous from a thousand throats!
But oh! how much more pleasing to behold,
The intellectual faculties unfold.
To see our children at a tender age,

Court learning and the sciences engage;
To see their infant geniuses arise,
And onward press to win the tempting prize!
To see them labour in the rugged field
Of grammar, and make that dry science yield.
In Geography all should excel,
Since it describes the globe on which we dwell,
Points out its countries, rivers, and its mines,
Where commerce most abounds, and gold most shines.
Geology, with persevering eye,
Traces the wreck of ages long gone by;
And clearly proves that this revolving earth,
Is now a million ages from her birth!
Who, though her parts have felt the hand of time,
Increase in beauty, and grow more sublime.
This botanist can prove, who love to trace
The splendid gems that ornament her face;
Whose business is with trees, plants, and flowers,
With fields and gardens, and arcadian bowers;
To trace their class, their order, and their tribe,
Their properties, and gender to describe,
And show how flowers, though not allowed to rove,
Breathe amorous fires, and burn in secret love;—
Teach how the females languish for the male,
And breathe their sighs in every scented gale;
And how the male in pity to his miss,
With the returning gale sends back a kiss!
Her gentle bosom feels the soft embrace,
And bears an offspring of superior grace.
Delightful science! formed not to perplex,
And well adapted to the lovely sex,
Who here may exercise their gentle powers,
And revel in the luxury of flowers!
Note every plant, their order and their class,
From the tall cedar to the humble grass;
Our ladies may, by such a bold advance,
Excel the daughters of our rival—France:
Whose artificial flow'rs in form and hue,
Resemble nature so exact and true;
In every line and fibre so complete,
That bees, deceived, strive to extract their sweet.
   But oh! how lamentable to behold,
A nation so ingenious and so bold,
Where every thing is twisted, turned and twirled,
To give the fashions to the civil world;
And who in nature's cause appear so warm
Should so distort creation's loveliest form!
Why is she in the stays of torture laced,
But to procure a long thin ugly waist?
Which checks the circulation, stops the breath,
And is the cause of frequent sudden death!
And oh, neglect not heavenly music's sounds,

Which calm the mind, and heal the bosom's wounds;
Call down glad spirits from the blessed abodes,
And soothe the passions of the angry gods!
Urania, too, should occupy our cares,
Whose voice awakes the music of the spheres!
While the celestial orbs with light sublime,
March through eternity and measure time,
Proclaiming as they roll through boundless space,
"Where harmony is not, there is no peace!"
And shall those lessons which the stars supply,
Be deemed too trifling to attract the eye?
Shall we despise the universal plan,
To gape and listen to pedantic man?
Forbid it genius, common sense, and pride,
Take nature for your school-master and guide;
For nature can alone the truth declare,
And make all objects with our reason square;
Try every science, humble and sublime,
No loss can be compared to loss of time!
   The theatres would be efficient schools,
Were they conducted with superior rules,
Made to reform, and guide the public taste,
And sanction nothing vicious and unchaste;
But while dramatic writers shall prefer,
To dramatize the Newgate Calendar;
And while Jack Shepherds' shall their pens engage,
And Toms' and Jerrys' stagger on the stage,
What have we to expect, but manners rude,
A gasping, grinning, noisy multitude?
The stage should far before the crowd advance,
To banish, not to cherish ignorance!
Pursue that course which virtue shall indite,
Not pander to a grovelling appetite;
Should lead the people on, not skulk behind,
And furnish plans to aid the vicious mind;
Its voice should thunder in the public cause,
Whether the meed were hisses or applause;
Without such independentcy the stage
May please the crowd, but ne'er can charm the sage.
   Nor does the pulpit much improve the plan,
In giving knowledge to its pupil, man,
Since no two sects can cordially agree,
And practice universal charity;
Without which all instruction is, alas!
Like tinkling cymbal, or like sounding brass.
For why is knowledge taught but to improve
Our charity, benevolence, and love?
Love, justice, truth, and charity of thought,
Was the pure doctrine that the Saviour taught;
And so the Church must teach, and lay aside
Her pomp and cant, intolerance and pride,
Or she from her false glory will be hurled,

And fall unpitied by a scorning world!
 Name not the bar! that dark unholy place,
Where man is taught his nature to disgrace;
Taught to declare on honor! at a time,
He knows his client's guilty of the crime,
That he believes the wretch is innocent,
And urges on the jury to consent,
To perjury! by swearing false is true,
To rob the gibbet of its lawful due.
Ah! will it be believed! the very words
The counsel spoke were echoed by the lords;
"Not guilty on my honor!" with loud cheers,
And Cardigan's acquitted by his peers!
The *moral lesson*, sanctioned by the lords,
Is now a precedent on their records,
Such are our courts, where honour's sold and bought,
Such are the schools in which our sons are taught!
These are thy fruits hereditary right,
Thy very breath creates a moral blight;
Through every rank the dire infection flies,
And weeping virtue mourns where honour dies.
Nor are the guardians of the public weal
More virtuous, or more disposed to feel
The moral degradation of the state,
Or they would a new destiny create—
Remould the institutions, or make new,
And render to the people what is due.
Instead of which they dastardly unite,
To trample on the poor, and crush their right;
To plunder labour of her daily bread,
And send her children supperless to bed.
And should one rise to advocate the poor,
The various animals set up a roar,
And cat-calls, grunts, cock-crows, and asses' brays,
Drown every word the unheard speaker says.
Is this the wisdom of the college clan?
Are those the men to rule their fellow man?
Who, whether from the *Isis* or the *Cam*,
Prove clear that *college learning* is but sham;
Though educated at a vast expence,
They never learnt good manners and good sense.
 And other institutions might be named,
More for their vices than their virtues famed,
Where pious men bequeathed their surplus store,
To educate the children of the poor;
But now the pampered bastards of the great,
Usurp those charities, and dissipate
Those funds, left by the dead whose spirit cry
"Vile sacrilege!" to every passer by.
 But 'tis the scientific institute
That claims our notice most, whose golden fruit
Is so congenial to the human mind,

That it should be the school of all mankind.
There knowledge is by every method sought,
And those who teach are anxious to be taught;
All mutually their sentiments impart,
And love of learning burns in every heart!
There heav'n-born truth is soberly pursued,
And prejudice and error stand subdued;
No old opinions are allowed to rest,
'Till they are weighed, and triumph o'er the test.
New lights are poured into the human soul,
Which make the passions easier to controul;
Through a new course the stream of knowledge runs
And sires receive instruction from their sons!
As to the earth, the rains in showers descend,
And stately rivers to the ocean wend,
And mountain streams rush headlong down the steep
To pay their tribute to the mighty deep;
So infant schools, though taught by village dames,
Are sources of the tributary streams,
That feed each little self-supporting college,
Which swell the flood of scientific knowledge;
And if the government would lend a hand,
Old England would become a classic land;
And mental beauties crowned with moral charms,
Would rise superior to a world in arms,
And human reason free and unconfined,
Would reign triumphant o'er a world of mind!
Those who instruct and train the rising youth,
In nature's laws, in science, and in truth,
And patronize self-educating schools,
And burst the bonds of antiquated rules,
To give a virtuous bias to the mind,
Are the best friends and patrons of mankind!
And such was he, that now extinguished star,
Who to the sons of science near and far
Gave light and life, and to the human will,
The grand momentum of mechanic skill.
In learning sage, in manners ever mild,
The tender father of a first born child;*
Or if not founder of that institute,
He breathed upon the germ and gave it root;
And which beneath his eye and fostering hand,
Has spread its branches over all the land!
Yes, such was Birkbeck! in whose master mind,
Philanthropy and science were combined;
He found the world in darkness when he came,
And kindled in our breasts a mental flame,
Which shall extend and unextinguished burn,
And be a light to ages yet unborn!
Then sing, oh, weeping Muse! his death deplore,
The bright, the generous Birkbeck is no more!

*The Mechanics Institute.

And there is *one*, the Muse with joy could name,
Whose modest genius shrinks from public fame;
But 'tis a duty kindred spirits feel,
The virtues of their fellows to reveal;
For though all private worth is public good,
'Tis public fame that leads the multitude;
And 'tis with pride I mention *Tower Street*,
Where youth and age, and male and female meet
To listen to the genius of the place,
And find their knowledge daily to increase.
The zealous Founder of that institute,
Who makes the sciences his grand pursuit,
And on all subjects takes enlightened views,
Deserves the praises of an abler Muse.
To see the noble work of his own hand,
Increase in numbers, and so firmly stand;
And his instruction, free and unconfined,
Awake the genius of the youthful mind,
Is to his feelings a more sweet reward
Than all the panegyrics of the bard.
The properties of light and heat are taught,
And miracles in chemistry are wrought;
While demonstration, by her stern decree,
Strikes home conviction and we all agree.
And logic with its *therefore* and its *why*,
And optics, which so oft deceive the eye;
As colours are well known to cheat the sight,
So different men see in a different light;
One calls an object blue, another green,
A third declares it is a shade between;
And being positive he wonders how
They could mistake in such a simple view.
Nor can the eye of *faith*, if we reflect,
Than the external eye, be more correct;
Nay, if we may judge by some people's creed,
The eye of faith is very blind indeed,
Or why do zealots their opponents spurn,
And joy to see their victims hang or burn!
Not so with science! she by nature's laws,
Examines the effect to find the cause;
Her high tribunal issues no decree,
Till on the verdict all the world agree!
And so religion should be purified,
And meek humility be made its guide;
Then all mankind united may behold
One faithful Shepherd! and one peaceful fold.

Pictoria;
or,
The Origin of Painting.

Almighty love! to thee we bend the knee,
Our choicest, sweetest blessings flow from thee;
To thee we owe our happiness on earth,
To thee all living creatures owe their birth;
To thee the poet owes his brightest themes,
To thee the virgin owes her happiest dreams,—
To thee the elegance of life we owe,
From which the arts of peace and science flow.
Thy everlasting flame can souls inspire,
And kindle in the breast the holy fire
Of pure affection— that celestial glow
Which none but thy true votaries can know.
'Twas thou that heldst the blazing torch, and
Though executed by a female hand, plann'd,
The grand design, when in her father's hall,
The fair Pictoria trac'd upon the wall,
While gentle spirits round breathed love and peace,
The shadow of her sleeping lover's face;
By which she saw, with rapture and delight,
That he, though absent, still might bless her sight!
The youth awoke—the shadow changed its place,
But left the outline of a beauteous face.
The blushing maiden hastened to remove
The bold confession of her virgin love,
But Theodore, in ecstacy of bliss,
Seized her soft hand, and stopped her with a kiss.
The happy father of the lovely maid,
With wonder and surprise, beheld the shade,
Kissed the fair hand that had contrived to trace
The faint resemblance of her lover's face,
And treasured up the image in his heart
'Twas the first inspiration of the art
And, however genius may it yet improve,
The bold invention sprang from woman's love;
From that the almost breathing canvass warms
To that the queen of beauty owes her charms.
And thou, Madonna! so serene and mild
Presenting to our view the holy child;
The grand creation that imparts delight,
And awful deluge that appals the sight!
All that is good in marble or in paint,
Whether a god, a goddess, or a saint,
All that has been produced by painting—all
Came from the shadow traced upon the wall.

The King of the Barricades.

I am King of the French,
  No one can deny.
And my name is Louis Phil,
  Though my subjects oft cry, Liberty,
I bend them to my will;
  For I have played a crafty game,
And passed through all the grades,
  And in July thirty I became,
The King of the Barricades.

My dad was old *egality*,
  And the idol of the mob,
While I was in reality,
  The man for any job;
And so I am resolved to be,
  Where'er my genius leads,
That all the world may clearly see,
  I am King of the Barricades.

With Kellerman and Dumouriez,
  I wore the crimson cap,
And bravely fought for liberty,
  At *Valmy* and *Genappe!*
But when my father lost his head,
  As many more had done,
I no more dreamt, for hope had fled,
  About the vacant throne.

I quickly cut the *tri-colors*,
  And the republic band,
For fifty thousand *louisd'ors*,
  From fair Penthievres hand!
I wandered over many a land,
  And practised many trades,
But now half Europe I command,
  I am King of the Barricades.

My voice was always for reform,
  But kept myself concealed,
Till Paris raised the civil storm,
  And then I stood revealed—
I bribed the rich, and crushed the poor,
  Gold eloquently pleads,
Still I have got great wealth in store,
  I am King of the Barricades.

I bothered poor old Lafayette,
  So well I played my card,
'Tis he wins most who best can cheat,
  And put men off their guard!

I scarcely could forbear to laugh,
  Amidst my own brigades,
When I became the golden calf,
  The King of the Barricades.

The *oriflame* I have unfurled,
  Against the daring press,
And every monarch in the world,
  Depends on my success;
My capital is fortified,
  With forts and palisades,
To keep my subjects down—besides,
  I am King of the Barricades.

I am resolved to persevere,
  And dare the bravo's knife,
My slaves shall see I feel no fear,
  I wear a charmed life;
In spite of that republic cry,
  That every where pervades,
My son shall reign when I shall die
  The King of the Barricades.

[Dedicated to The Midnight Dream]

To Mr. T. Cooper, the Chartist Poet.

SIR,

In gratitude for the favours I have received through your kindly feeling towards me, who am almost a stranger to you, and for the many good qualities that you are known to possess, I have endeavoured in the shape of a *Dream*, to form and estimate of your poetical merit, in the following complimentary little poem; but I have dicovered that my poetical genius is totally inadequate to do justice to the transcendant abilities you have evinced in the composition of your immortal poem the *Purgatory of Suicides*. I have not read it all, but I have read enough to know that such a poem could emenate from no common mind. The passage describing the unfortunate "Sapho," is at once beautiful and sublime.

I now, Sir, beg you to accept the poetical trifle, as the humble production of,

Sir,
Your much obliged friend,
ALLEN DAVENPORT.

75, Noble Street, Goswell Street,
July 6th, 1846.

The Midnight Dream.

Methought 'twas midnight, and the glorious skies,
Were veiled from all but philosophic eyes;
While others slumber sages pant for fame,
And night and day alike young poets dream
Of goddesses, and nymphs, and flowery vales,
And paint on fancy's web sweet fairy tales;
For poetry can every passion move,
Like the enchantments of fond woman's love!
Thus bards, who see where vulgar eyes are blind,
Rush on and leave the multitude behind.
'Tis said that Orpheus, with his magic song,
Made forests dance and drew the rocks along;
And with his lyre broke the infernal spell,
And call'd his *Eurydice* back from hell!
But 'tis a modern Orpheus that claims,
Interpretation of my midnight dreams.
Wrapt in a mistic robe I gazed around,
And from the centre of the dark profound,
A pale and glimmering light broke from afar,
'Twas like the shadowy twilight of a star;
And while I look'd upon the flickering gloom,
As from a dungeon or a living tomb,
I saw a spirit, bursting into light,
And chasing far away the shades of night;
His glorious track became a milky-way,
Which soon extended into boundless day!
'Twas heavenly genius! with a golden pen,
Come to write "TRUTH" upon the hearts of men!
The world awoke—from its profound repose,
A shout was heard—a monument arose;
On whose broad base, wrote with a hand sublime,
In burning characters—"*A Prison Rhyme!*"
Another—and another shout was heard,
And every eye was fixed upon the bard.
And critics and reviewers from all parts,
Engravers—painters—all the sister arts,
While the vast crowd all anxious to behold,
Wrote on the monument in burnished gold,
The name of "*Cooper!*" now a deathless name,
The child of genius—and the *pet* of fame!
Another shout! ten thousand voices broke,
Upon my startled ear, and I awoke.

The Showman.

I'm an orator, and my name is Broom,
On the banks of the Thames in a splendid room,
I am master of a raree show,
Where may noble automotons stand in view;
And every one performs his part,
Just as if he had brain and a human heart,
With my *Rege, Lege, Grege O*,
Walk in, walk in, to my raree show.

I lately took a trip to France,
To perfect myself in the Polka Dance,
Where the natives all were amazed to see,
My prowess of Terpsichore;
And the English too shall shortly know,
I can dance as well as jump Jim Crow,
With my *Rege, Lege, Grege O*,
Walk in, walk in, to my raree show.

But I have a dance that is newer still,
Than either Polka or Quadrille,
'Tis call'd the *Woolsack*, which 'tis known,
Is but one step from the royal throne,
For I know the Duke will my suit advance,
And patronize the Woolsack dance;
With my *Rege, Lege, Grege O*,
Walk in, walk in, to my raree show.

In the show I shall make many a speech,
Lord! how my hands and feet will itch,
To show the world my matchless skill,
In gilding of a legal pill;
And the very shadow of my nose
Will scare away my boldest foes;
With my *Rege, Lege, Grege O*,
Walk in, walk in, to my raree show.

[Editor's note: The subject of this poem is Lord Brougham, Lord Chancellor 1830–1834.]

From, *The Origin of Man and the Progress of Society* (1846)

I Origin of Language and Private Property

After discovering the advantages of tillage and cultivation, which would supply food, for themselves and provender for their cattle, each family having plenty of materials, would inclose their little domain, and consider it private property, and the law of trespass would commence. The law of *meum et tuum*, or mine and thine, was enacted, has been the basis of all the systems, governments, and institutions that have been established in the world, and is the chief cause of the wars and despotism which have afflicted mankind.

However, everything went on progressing till men became little landowners, each cultivating his own estate, and managing his own affairs; and a sort of equality reigned in the unpretending rural community. But at length it so happened that some who had cultivated pieces of land with much care and great labour must needs sell, or barter away, their land for some consideration, which would soon be dissipated, and the fruits of their labour lost for ever; while the purchaser of the land was laying the foundation of a system of injustice and oppression that world has never yet been able to overturn – a system that has blunted the finer feelings destroyed all the milder virtues, and nearly extinguished those social sympathies which suffering humanity claims at the hands of civil society.

The system of buying and selling land being established, the principle of *lord* and *slave* followed as an inevitable consequence. The land, which was common to the whole human race before, now becomes individualised, and made private property; and those who held the land usurped the power of making the laws, of establishing the institutions, and forming the social arrangements by which they held the power of *life and death* over the landless portion of society. This power created an aristocracy and monarchy; and those who had no land, and consequently no power to protect their honest labour, became the *helots* of the state, and a system of rich and poor, oppression and tyranny, poverty and suffering, became hereditary in every nation of the earth!

In the course of time the nations of husbandmen, as I shall call them, were enabled to produce more wealth than they could, or were permitted to consume, and a system of barter, the harbinger of general commerce, soon followed. But men discovering that immense fortunes could quickly be made by success in commercial pursuits, the land, which is the foundation of all wealth and power, became neglected; and some states, after having accumulated much wealth, and acquired great renown, turned their backs upon nature, as it were, departed from her laws, created for themselves an artificial state, and called it civilisation.

The people now assumed an entire new character; the simple manners and innocent amusements to which our rude but honest ancestors had been so long accustomed were laid aside, and new customs were introduced. The political and moral systems of the world became corrupted, vice stalked abroad in naked deformity, depravity reigned in every rank, and oppression, fraud, and murder, became every day occurrences; and gaols, whipping posts, and gibbets, were the prominent ornaments of civilised states, for such crimes were committed, that were never heard nor dreamt of in the pristine state of society.

II Currency – Commerce – Monopoly

The discovery of steam power has completely changed the aspect of human affairs, and caused such a stupendous revolution in the production and distribution of wealth, that the mind is perplexed and bewildered in contemplating their vast increase. . . . Yet strange anomaly! honest and industrious people in this country are wasting away through want of common necessaries of life, and die, annually by sheer starvation; yet people persist in calling this murderous state of things civilisation.

By what means have the few been enabled to accumulate such enormous masses of wealth, while the toiling millions, with their utmost exertions, are doomed to suffer the greatest privations? By monopoly! first in the land, which is the foundation of all other monopolies. *It* has ruined the small farmer and the agricultural labourer; it destroys every prospect of the farmer by oppressive rents, game laws, and other tyrannical regulations, the evils of which descend to the labourer, and prevent him from obtaining an honest and comfortable subsistence when in full employment. As a natural consequence, when out of work, he turns poacher, and makes war upon my lord's game, and gets transported. Or should he abstain from such a course of life, he is compelled, by sheer necessity, to break up his little home, and go with all his wretched family into a union bastille to break stones for three farthings a bushel!

The monopoly of capital is doing the same thing by the small trader and his assistants, by destroying the profits of the master and reducing the wages of the servant. The monopoly of machinery is degrading, and starving the ingenious mechanic out of existence, by superseding manual labour by an unconsuming power – a power with which no human exertions can compete. The monopoly of the church has deprived the poor of the means which their pious and benevolent forefathers had bequeathed, and devoted to the education of their children, and to the support of the aged and infirm; and which also keep the lower order of the clergy in a state of poverty and degradation, while the great dignitaries of the church loll in their chariots and fare sumptuous every day. All these monopolies have created a monster in the state in the shape of Class Legislation, productive of the most serious injustice, over which the great mass of the people have not the slightest control.

The Land, the People's Farm

The God of nature at his birth,
Gave man his title to the earth;
Then let us show our title deed,
United, and we shall succeed;
And prove, if need, with our right arm,
The land, the land's the people's farm.

All were supplied with daily bread,
'Till proud usurpers raised their head;
Who trampled on the law Divine,
And substituted "*Mine*" and "*Thine*",
Which through the world spread dire alarm
They robbed the people of their farm.

Unite! Unite!! for God decrees,
Though Justice works by slow degrees;
That all the land shall be restored;
And God is faithful to his word;
The day and hour is now at hand,
To repossess the stolen land.

The savage has his freehold home,
And hunting park wherein to roam;
No laws of 'trespass' there restrain,
The child of nature scorns the chain;
No 'Game preserves' spread o'er the land,
All game is free to every hand.

Shall Christian governments destroy,
Those rights which savages enjoy;
And reign supreme o'er field and flood,
And traffic with the people's blood!
Oh no! the millions now must make a stand,
And add to the Charter, their claim to the land.

[Northern Star, 27 June 1846]

Further reading and bibliography of secondary literature

Further reading

Considerable information about Davenport can be found in the major secondary literature about metropolitan radicalism. Iorwerth Prothero's *Artisans and Politics* is the only book to cover all the political movements in which Davenport was involved. It should be read in conjunction with three more-recent works: *London Chartism* by David Goodway; Malcolm Chase, '*The People's Farm*'; and Iain McCalman's *Radical Underworld*. The latter is an indispensible guide to the literary world inhabited by Davenport.

There is an entry for Davenport, and a complete bibliography of his published writings, in volume eight of the *Dictionary of Labour Biography* edited by Bellamy and Saville. This volume also contains entries for his closest political associates: Thomas Spence, Thomas Evans, Charles Neesom, Robert Wedderburn and Thomas Preston. The best starting-point to discover more about G. J. Harney is Schoyen's biography *Chartist Challenge*. J. F. C. Harrison, *Learning and Living* remains the best study of adult education in the period. David Vincent's *Bread, Knowledge and Freedom* is a seminal study of the genre of working-class autobiography.

Bibliography of secondary literature

Bellamy, Joyce and John Saville (eds) (1987), *Dictionary of Labour Biography, 8*, London: Macmillan.

Bennett, Jennifer (1982), 'The London Democratic Association 1837–1841: A Study in London Radicalism', in J. Epstein and D. Thompson (eds.), *The Chartist Experience: Studies in Working-Class Radicalism and Culture, 1830–60*, London: Macmillan.

Burnett, J., Vincent, D. and Mayall, D. (eds) (1984), *The Autobiography of the Working Class: An Annotated, Critical Bibliography – Volume One: 1790–1900*, Brighton: Harvester Press.

Chase, Malcolm (1988), *'The People's Farm': English Radical Agrarianism, 1775–1840*, Oxford: Oxford University Press.

Claeys, Gregory (1989), *Citizens and Saints: Politics and Anti-Politics in Early British Socialism*, Cambridge: Cambridge University Press.

Claeys, Gregory (1987), *Machinery, Money and the Millennium: from Moral Economy to Socialism*, Cambridge: Polity Press.

Fleishman, Avrom (1983), *Figures of Autobiography: the Language of Self-Writing in Victorian and Modern England*, Berkeley: University of California Press.

Gagnier, Regenia (1987), 'Social atoms: working-class autobiography, subjectivity and gender', *Victorian Studies 30*, 3.

Goldstein, Leonard (1984), 'A Handlist of Nineteenth Century Working Class Fiction and Some Related Materials', *Wissenschaftliche Zeitschrift* [Potsdam], 28.

Goodway, David (1984a), *London Chartism*, Cambridge: Cambridge University Press.

Goodway, David (1984b), 'The Métivier Collection and the books of George Julian Harney', *Bulletin of the Society for the Study of Labour History* 49.

Green, S. J. D. (1990), 'Religion and the rise of the Common Man: Mutual Improvement Societies, Religious Associations and Popular Education in Three Industrial Towns in the West Riding of Yorkshire, c. 1850–1900', in Derek Fraser (ed.), *Cities, Class and Communication: Essays in Honour of Asa Briggs*, Hassocks: Harvester Press.

Hambrick, Margaret (1986), *A Chartist's Library*, London: Mansell.

Harrison, J. F. C. (1961), *Learning and Living: A Study in the History of the English Adult Education Movement*, London: Routledge Kegan Paul.

Harrison, Royden (1961), 'Labour notes and queries: Allen Davenport', *Bulletin of the Society for the Study of Labour History* 2, spring.

Kirk, Neville (1985), *The Growth of Working Class Reformism*, London: Croom Helm.

McCalman, Iain (1988), *Radical Underworld: Prophets, Revolutionaries and Pornographers in London, 1795–1840*, Cambridge: Cambridge University Press.

McCalman, Iain (ed.), (1991), *The Horrors of Slavery and Other Writings by Robert Wedderburn*, Edinburgh: Edinburgh University Press.

Mansfield, Nick (1979), 'John Brown: A Shoemaker in Place's London', *History Workshop Journal* 8, autumn.

Olney, James (ed.) (1988), *Studies in Autobiography*, New York: Oxford University Press.

Pascal, Roy (1960), *Design and Truth in Autobiography*, London: Routledge Kegan Paul.

Prothero, Iorwerth (1978), *Artisans and Politics in Early Nineteenth Century London: John Gast and His Times*, Folkestone: Dawson.

Prothero, Iorwerth (1979) 'Allen Davenport (1775–1846)', in *Biographical Dictionary of Modern British Radicals, vol. 1*, ed. J. O. Baylen and N. J. Gossmann, Brighton: Harvester Press.

Radcliffe, C. J. (1986), 'Mutual Improvement Societies in the West Riding of Yorkshire, 1835–1900', *Journal of Educational Administration and History, 13* (2), July.

Schoyen, A. R. (1958) *The Chartist Challenge: A Portrait of George Julian Harney*, London: Heinemann.

Shepard, Leslie (1969), *John Pitts: Ballad printer of Seven Dials, London, 1765–1844*, London: Library Association.

Sturrock, John (1993), *The Language of Autobiography: Studies in the First Person Singular*, Cambridge: Cambridge University Press.

Thompson, Dorothy (1971), *The Early Chartists*, London: Macmillan.

Thompson, E. P. (1968), *The Making of the English Working Class*, 2nd edn, Harmondsworth: Penguin Books.

Thurston, Gavin (1967), *The Clerkenwell Riot: the Killing of Constable Culley*, London: George Allen & Unwin.

Vincent, David (1977), *Testaments of Radicalism: Memoirs of Working Class Politicians, 1790–1885*, London: Europa.

Vincent, David (1981), *Bread, Knowledge and Freedom: A Study of Nineteenth-Century Working Class Autobiography*, London: Europa.

Williams, Gwyn (1965), *Rowland Detrosier: A Working-Class Infidel, 1830–34*, York: Borthwick Institute for Historical Research.

Index